LIFE'S
A
POOCH

LIFE'S A POOCH

QUOTES ABOUT DOGS
BY PEOPLE WHO LOVE THEM

BOZE HADLEIGH

Skyhorse Publishing

Skyhorse Publishing books may be purchased in bulk at special discounts for sales promotion, corporate gifts, fund-raising, or educational purposes. Special editions can also be created to specifications. For details, contact the Special Sales Department, Skyhorse Publishing, 307 West 36th Street, 11th Floor, New York, NY 10018 or info@skyhorsepublishing.com.

Skyhorse® and Skyhorse Publishing® are registered trademarks of Skyhorse Publishing, Inc.®, a Delaware corporation.

Visit our website at www.skyhorsepublishing.com.

10 9 8 7 6 5 4 3 2 1

Library of Congress Cataloging-in-Publication Data is available on file.

Jacket design by Rain Saukas
Jacket photographs: iStockphoto
Interior illustrations by Val Khislavsky

Print ISBN: 978-1-5107-2470-9
Ebook ISBN: 978-1-5107-2471-6

Printed in China

Dedicated to Ronnie, to the memory of Pooch—
young and old, she learned new tricks—
and to those who cherish and protect sentient beings.

Contents

Introduction

One can live happily without a dog. But one can live more happily with a dog.

Does any other nonhuman begin to match a dog's desire to bond with its human companion? There's so much that can be said about dogs—and in this book, here's a lot of it!

Dog talk typically results in a smile. It can also surprise or inform us, sometimes for the betterment of our four-legged friend via practical tips and advice. Occasionally it shocks us, for not everybody loves dogs. Or for that matter, animals.

But even in dog-friendly cultures it's true that we are their voice. Like children, dogs and other pets are at the mercy of their owners. Fortunately, dogs are generally loved and spoiled as never before. Modern society has a higher regard and concern for animals than our ancestors did. Affluence, education, and increased leisure helped make this possible.

For decades I've read about the pooch-person bond, canines in civilization, and how dogs shape us and we shape them (even literally). But my biggest realization of how dog-minded we are came while researching the opening canine chapter of *Holy Cow!: Doggerel, Catnaps, Scapegoats, Foxtrots & Horse Feathers*, my book about animal words, phrases, epithets, and expressions. Only the horse competes with the dog in language references—from hot dogs, dog days, underdog, a dogsbody, hangdog, and dog star to lucky dog, dog-eat-dog, a dog's life, in the dog house, hair of the dog, seeing a man about a dog, going to the dogs, dog tags, dog in the manger, my dogs are killing me, dogfish, dog paddle, doggy bag, houndstooth, publicity hound (several in this book!), hush puppies, puppy love, pup tent, barking up the wrong tree, a shaggy dog story, a bone to pick, cur, chow, pooch, bitch, mutt (derives from sheep; i.e., muttonhead), and umpteen more.

Life's a Pooch is divided into chapters spotlighting the dog's role as a best pal, a pampered pet, a big- and little-screen darling, and a cultural icon, plus a chapter giving equal time (not too much!) to those who prefer cats—or neither. Sources include books, newspapers, and magazines in five languages, the Internet to a lesser extent, as well as personal interviews and several generous dog lovers who opened doors to others who gave me more canine quotes, some of whom then did the same, until after almost two decades there was enough to fill a book.

Media coverage of personalities is typically me-me-me, but hopefully the exclusive status of many of these quotes provides a glimpse into the less emphasized sphere of celebrity love for dogs. Almost nobody who lives with a pooch isn't willing—nay, eager—to share that dog in words.

So, please enjoy . . . and why not follow Betty White's suggestion to read this with your best friend on your lap or by your side, preferably aloud. After all, your voice is one of the things your dog loves about you. Arf!

Boze Hadleigh
Beverly Hills, CA
May 15, 2017

Chapter 1

EVERYONE'S
BEST FRIEND
(A PET AND A PAL)

Happiness is a warm puppy.

—CHARLES M. SCHULZ, creator of *Peanuts*

If you want to be happy for seven years, get married. If you want to be happy for fifteen years, get a dog. If you want to be happy for a lifetime, take up gardening.

—MARTHA STEWART, lifestyle guru

For me, happiness is a little white two-pound Chihuahua named Minnie the Mouse. Allow yourself the luxury of letting happiness be whatever it is to you. And for some of us, a puppy or a dog we love is pure joy. May that special joy find its way into your heart and keep you warm.

—DANIELLE STEELE, bestselling novelist

The phrase "man's best friend" is an understatement. More like a devoted platonic lover.

—MELISSA MCCARTHY, actress

God, or Mother Nature, made a big mistake by letting people live so much longer than dogs and cats. Or should I say, by making dogs and cats live so much shorter than the people who love them.

— BRAD PITT, actor

Such short little lives our pets have to spend with us, and they spend most of it waiting for us to come home each day.

— JOHN GROGAN, author

One hears repeatedly about man's best friend. We place the dog on a pedestal because it's friendly and loyal to us. "Man's best friend, man's best friend." I'm more interested in being my dog's best friend.

— ADELE, singer-songwriter

I cannot quantify how much hope and comfort I found looking into [my late white Poodle] Sadie's eyes over her lifetime. . . . She was given to me as a puppy, an unexpected gift. I will always miss her.

— BARBRA STREISAND, singer and actress

Once you have had a wonderful dog, a life without one is a life diminished.

—DEAN KOONTZ, author

🐾 🐾 🐾

Dogs are not our whole life, but they make our lives whole.

—ROGER A. CARAS, host of the annual
Westminster Kennel Club

🐾 🐾 🐾

Your dog belongs to you. But sometimes stop and think that you belong to your dog.

—JENNIFER BEALS, actress (*Flashdance*)

🐾 🐾 🐾

After my husband Joey died, Jazzy became the love of my life. I never knew so much love could come from such a small package.

—CINDY ADAMS, columnist and author
of two books about Jazzy, her Yorkie

People ask why I conduct an orchestra with a Chihuahua in my other hand. Because it gives me confidence and affection, and fits in my hand or pocket. I have had several wives and Chihuahuas, but only my little dogs are portable.

— XAVIER CUGAT, Spanish American bandleader

*   *   *

I went to a pet store to window-shop for a dog. I did some research and found out small dogs tend to live longer, so I was set on a small dog. But I liked all the dogs I saw! So I did some more research. I found out not to go to a pet store that might be mixed up with puppy mills; go instead to the local pound or shelter. I did, and now I have a true best friend.

— RUE MCCLANAHAN, actress (*Golden Girls*)

*   *   *

There are three faithful friends: an old wife, an old dog, and ready money.

— BENJAMIN FRANKLIN, statesman

You go to an animal shelter and there are all these wonderful dog and cat faces, and some are looking right at you, and then you see one that keeps on looking at you, and it moves toward you and wants your attention . . . meanwhile you stand there staring and relating, and something passes between you, and *that's* the pet for you. It's just meant to be.

—LINDSAY LOHAN, actress

Finding exactly the right dog is a lot like falling in love. But almost never as risky or with an I-should-have-known-better ending.

—RENEE ZELLWEGER, actress

A lover will tell you how terrific you are with words. But words are so easy. Dogs tell you with their very selves, repeatedly and consistently.

—KATE MOSS, supermodel

Don't accept your dog's admiration as conclusive evidence that you are wonderful.

—ANN LANDERS, advice columnist

To his dog, every man is Napoleon, hence the constant popularity of dogs.

—ALDOUS HUXLEY, author

*   *   *

The better I get to know men, the more I find myself loving dogs.

—CHARLES DE GAULLE, former president of France

*   *   *

If you want a friend in Washington, get a dog.

—HARRY S. TRUMAN, former president
of the United States

*   *   *

If you pick up a starving dog and make him prosperous, he will not bite you. This is the principal difference between a dog and a man.

—MARK TWAIN, author and humorist

*   *   *

The average dog is a nicer person than the average person.

—ANDY ROONEY, humorist

— ⊙ ⊙ —

Dogs are also a woman's best friend—more of a friend than a man. After all, a dog stays for life.

—BRIGITTE BARDOT, former French sex symbol

🐾 🐾 🐾

The more boys I meet, the more I love my dog.

—CARRIE UNDERWOOD, singer-songwriter

🐾 🐾 🐾

Men call women they consider unattractive dogs, which is a double put-down to women and to dogs. For my money, most dogs are more attractive than most men. And faithful? Don't make me laugh.

—LISA LAMPANELLI, comedian

🐾 🐾 🐾

A dog will never tell you to shut up.

—MARILYN MONROE, legend

Dogs are better than human beings because they know but do not tell.

> —EMILY DICKINSON, poet

Dogs are smarter than lots of people. They wag their tails instead of their tongue.

> —JERRY SEINFELD, actor and comedian

Believe it or not, I had a dog that loved cheesecake. So did my ex-husband. Only he liked the kind you chase. The guy was also a lush. Thank goodness dogs never become alcoholics. The only thing they're addicted to is their masters, bless their darling little hearts.

> —PHYLLIS DILLER, comedian and actress

A dog is the only friend you can have in life who will go with you wherever you want to go, whenever you want to go, without question, and without putting on his pants.

> —PADGETT POWELL, novelist and reviewer

Dogs don't betray you. That's a tremendous plus. What could be worse than someone you trust ending up betraying you? The worst you can say with pets is they might be fickle: if somebody comes along and gives them treats or meals, they'll gravitate in that direction. But wouldn't most humans do the same? And don't all children do that?

—JAMES GANDOLFINI, actor (*The Sopranos*)

🐾 🐾 🐾

Dogs are themselves. They're never phony. They're like people are before they reach puberty. What you see is what you get, and how dogs act is how they are.

—ZAC EFRON, actor

🐾 🐾 🐾

It's neat how dogs are dogs first and foremost. Not a sex. With humans, so much of our identity depends on what we wear and our hair, makeup, shoes. Dogs and cats are who they are without needing disguises, accessories, fetish clothing, jewelry, or rules on how to look and not look. Dogs are natural.

—HELEN HUNT, actress

To attract a man, you have to be pretty, pretty, pretty. I don't have time for that—I'm too busy cleaning my gun. It's so much more convenient for dogs. They don't go by looks, they go by animal attraction. Any shape, size, snout, ear length, tail type, or breed will do.

—HENRIETTE MANTEL, actress
(*The Brady Bunch Movie*)

Most dogs are cute. Very few are plain or ugly, and the great thing is, even if and when they are, dogs don't know it. . . . If animals were looks-conscious like people, they'd be more into themselves and give us that much less attention. Instead, dogs give themselves wholeheartedly to people. Fortunately for us egotistical humans.

—ELLEN DEGENERES, comedian and actress

I felt sorry when I went to a dog show because of all the value placed on their looks. People were constantly commenting on which dog looked better than the next. It doesn't matter to the dogs, so why should people be so concerned? Besides, dogs love us no matter what we look like.

—TYLER PERRY, author

I feel that dog shows are fun to look at, but rather pointless. Not to mention open to a judge's bias. To me, it's like the trophy wife concept—it's empty. You want a trophy marriage, not a trophy spouse. Likewise, every happy dog is already a champion, and it's your relationship with your canine companion that deserves the trophy.

— BETTY WHITE, actress and animal activist

🐾   🐾   🐾

I got a lot of flak when I once said I'd never enjoyed the depth of relationship with a human that I've had with dogs. Because I didn't make an exception of my son. But let's face it, kids grow up and away, and not just geographically. . . . Sons inhabit their own exclusive world after about age ten, and they usually don't want Mom around except for short visits and meals.

— DORIS DAY, founder of the Doris Day Animal League

🐾   🐾   🐾

Lots of women get over broken relationships with the help of their dogs. A dog is sympathetic, and taking care of it is like taking care of a child. It helps get your mind off the guy who done you wrong.

— CHELSEA HANDLER, talk-show host and author

— 🎾 —

When an eighty-five-pound mammal licks your tears away, then tries to sit on your lap, it's hard to feel sad.

—KRISTAN HIGGINS, romance novelist

* * *

If a dog jumps in your lap, it is because he is fond of you. If a cat does the same thing, it is because your lap is warmer.

—ALFRED NORTH WHITEHEAD,
mathematician and philosopher

* * *

Long ago I had this mean girlfriend. I only liked her for her looks . . . eventually that wasn't enough. When we broke up I finally called her a bitch because I wasn't going to get any more sex, so I didn't have to pretend she wasn't one. Then I went into this blue funk and through it all the companionship and devotion of my neighbor's Poodle Josette—my neighbor was away for the summer—kept me from sinking into deep depression. Before too long I came out of it and apologized to Josette. I told her I would never use the word "bitch" again because it was an insult to her and all other she-dogs.

—GENE RAYBURN, host of *Match Game*

People think because Poodles walk a certain way they aren't intelligent. As far as I know, they're the most intelligent dog there is. They're very loyal too. Remember, they don't choose to get trimmed a certain way—that's the owner's doing. So if a Poodle looks somewhat ridiculous, consider its owner. . . .

— FRANK MAYA, comedian

I wonder if other dogs think Poodles are members of a weird religious cult.

— RITA RUDNER, comedian and writer

Don't ask me why, I always wanted to have a Pekingese . . . just something about them. They're Chinese, and so is my name, but I changed it—it was Suzuki, which is Japanese. Professional reasons. . . . But a Pekingese is small and funny-looking and at that time I was too focused on what other people might think of me. Now I focus on what I think of other people.

— JACK SOO, actor (Barney Miller)

My family, when I was very young, was alarmed that for several birthdays I wanted a Great Dane. They thought such a dog was only for a boy or man. I thought it would be delightfully outlandish, a small girl with a big dog. Like something from a children's book illustration. And, in addition, I could ride it! But my family had the last word. *Then.*

— ASTRID LINDGREN, author of
the Pippi Longstocking books

🐾   🐾   🐾

Nothing lingers more achingly or longer in a little one's memory than the gift and love of a dog or cat that is later taken away. That should not happen to any child.

— MARY ROBINSON, former president of Ireland

🐾   🐾   🐾

When I was growing up the neighbors got a Collie for their son, who was thrilled. So was I, and jealous. Less than a year later they gave the dog away. I found out it was because they expected her to be another Lassie, to do tricks and act heroic or whatever. This dog was as nice and sweet as Lassie, but of course she wasn't a trained actor. What lousy neighbors! They could've asked *me*—I'd have taken that dog and really loved it.

— BRANDON deWILDE, actor (*Shane*)

Time heals all wounds. It also heels most hounds. And hopefully wounds all heels.

— BARBARA WOODHOUSE, British dog trainer

🐾 🐾 🐾

Do you know, when I was a kid I briefly had a dog I secretly called Craig, until it was returned to its true owner. . . . I still have a photo of Craig, but I never did find out Craig's gender. I didn't think to ask or look. I didn't care. I just loved Craig. And that Craig loved me.

— CRAIG CLAIBORNE, food critic

🐾 🐾 🐾

I thought it would be so cute and glamorous to have a dog tiny enough to carry around in my purse—my own constant companion and our own dash of complicity. Plus I'd pick beautiful purses to carry my doggie in. A few of the grown-up models were doing that. It might sound shallow for an adult, but not for a young miss.

— SANDRA DEE, teen model turned movie star

— 🎾 🎾 —

The thing about a dog is, thinking about yours you usually have a smile on your face or inside you.

—BILL CLINTON, former president of the United States

*   *   *

When I was younger and feeling kind of depressed, sex would sort of lighten my load. Very temporarily . . . and you often had to go looking for it. Time tends to even things out. Now I have a dog, I'm rarely depressed, and if I am, just sitting with and cuddling my dog usually takes it away.

—JACK LARSON, actor (Jimmy Olson on TV's *Superman*)

*   *   *

The pleasant but serious responsibility of taking care of my dog leaves less time for thinking more or too much about myself. It must be like parenting, only less noisy and expensive.

—LOUIS EDMONDS, actor (*Dark Shadows*)

If you tend to brood or overeat, get a child—preferably a grandchild—or a dog or cat or a time-consuming charity. Going outside yourself, keeping busy, that doesn't leave enough time to make depression a routine or food an excuse.

— VIRGINIA GRAHAM, talk-show host

※   ※   ※

As teenagers we look in the mirror too often comparing, which doesn't result in happiness. . . . We had a neighbor, Mr. Lewis, who owned possibly the ugliest dog I've ever seen. The only cute thing about her was her size, like a Yorkshire Terrier. But to this day I've no idea what breed the poor mutt was. No, Trudy wasn't a poor mutt! She was a cheery, energetic, lovable little creature. Everyone liked her, and Trudy sensed it. And of course she didn't know from mirrors. Thinking about Trudy makes me laugh, and I could almost cry. She absolutely inspired me.

— LIZABETH SCOTT, movie star (née Emma Matzo)

※   ※   ※

At a time when maintaining human connections seems to be more difficult, a four-legged family member can ease the loneliness and help us connect with other people.

— MARTY BECKER, veterinarian and TV personality

A virtuous thing about dogs is they don't necessarily get lonely and certainly don't have all the neuroses and hang-ups more and more people seem to have. When I was growing up I never heard of autism or anorexia, about AFD. Maybe all that existed, but not to the extent it does now. Whereas dogs are so uncomplicated.

— ANDY GRIFFITH, actor

🐾   🐾   🐾

No question that dogs do get lonely. At least modern dogs do. It could be from indoor living and over-reliance, emotionally and practically, on one or a few humans. . . . It seems as if dogs spend half their lives waiting for humans . . . waiting for attention.

— Dame JUDI DENCH, actress

🐾   🐾   🐾

Before cars and roads, the average dog was out and about, interacting with other dogs and other people. Now, to prevent getting hit by a vehicle, a dog is usually kept cooped up and away from other life forms.

— HARVEY MILK, San Francisco politician

— 🎾 🎾 —

A dog is always ready. It doesn't matter for what, dogs are just ready. If you leave your car window open, the dog will leap into the car and sit there for hours. The dog knows that sometimes the car just starts moving, and you have to be ready!

— DAVE BARRY, humorist

※　※　※

Dogs can be so happy with people, and they don't have fights with them, like happens so often between dogs . . . I know there are all these studies about how having a dog around improves your blood pressure and can extend your life. But I wonder if it's ever been studied how having a human in their life improves and extends the life of dogs and improves *their* blood pressure?

— ELLEN POMPEO, actress (*Grey's Anatomy*)

※　※　※

If I were a cat or dog, I'd definitely want to be a pet, I'd want to be owned. That means somebody has to take responsibility for you. . . . Imagine being a dog or cat out there, on your own in the urban jungle or in actual wilderness. Terrible. Terribly sad. Pets have better and longer lives, quite apart from enriching their owners' lives.

— MATT DAMON, actor

The measurably positive effect of pets on people is greatest on children and the elderly. In other words, on those with the most time on their hands. What better to fill spare time and an emotional void than a dog or cat?

—JOHN CLEESE, actor

For a lot of love in a smaller package, you can't beat a dog. It's some bargain.

—DWIGHT D. EISENHOWER,
former president of the United States

A small dog doesn't necessarily mean a small personality. What's inside a dog can't be measured in quantity.

—MERYL STREEP, actress-plus

Dogs request nothing from humans but food, affection, and consistency. In return, they give their all.

—LADY GAGA, singer and activist

It has been proven visually, reactively, and scientifically with monitoring machines that a person can be angry one moment and then, upon seeing a dog or type of dog they particularly like, spontaneously transfer into a good or even joyous mood within three seconds of seeing the dog.

—RITA LEVI-MONTALCINI,
neurophysiologist and Nobel Prize winner

❧ ❧ ❧

The biggest change in the animal–human relationship over the last few centuries is that dogs and cats in particular are now valued far more for psychological reasons than utilitarian ones. In past ages, a family pet had to earn its keep as a watchdog, a herder of livestock, a hunting enabler, or a sled puller . . . a mouser or a rat catcher. Today a pet simply has to love and be loved. Too bad our relations with fellow humans haven't evolved similarly.

—Dr. TIMOTHY LEARY, psychologist

❧ ❧ ❧

Some dogs just won't learn to play nice with other dogs. You can "whisper" or yell or train them all you want, but the only one benefiting is the "expert" you're paying. What matters is if the dog is nice to you and if you're nice to your dog.

—ANNE MEARA, actress, comedian,
and mother of Ben Stiller

In Europe, the nickname of the Pit Bull is "the nanny dog" because it is very good with children. It is not unfriendly where I come from. Only when I visited the USA did I hear that the dog has a bad reputation over there.

— PEDRO ALMODOVAR, director

A mean dog is that way because a mean person made it that way, through neglect or abuse or deliberate programming. Of course, some dogs have unpleasant personalities, as some people do. No explaining that!

— TAB HUNTER, former screen heartthrob

It's intriguing that the word "personality" was designed to reflect on people, yet some dogs have more personality than some persons.

— RITA MORENO, actress

You know what I love? Those stories about a cat or a dog that got lost, like on a family trip, and then they made their way back to their home and family hundreds or even thousands of miles away. It's incredible, but some of those stories are very well documented.

— KATE HUDSON, actress

It is a myth, and one wishes otherwise, that dogs have some type of homing instinct and can get lost, then invariably find their way back home. Most do not. If your dog gets lost, please don't assume it will soon return. Act immediately, because the longer your pet goes missing, the fewer the chances it will be returned safe and sound. Or alive.

— PORTER WASHINGTON, dog trainer and breeder

🐾   🐾   🐾

I was touched by a recent story about Ginger, a German Shepherd whose owner gave her up after he became homeless and couldn't afford her anymore. She was put in a shelter in Apple Valley, California, but escaped after getting through three doors, then jumping out the entrance to her freedom. Ginger didn't find her former home . . . she was located three days later, about three miles from the shelter. The happy ending for the dog, if not the homeless man, was that she was given a new home with new owners.

— GUS VAN SANT, director

I adopted a German Shepherd because they form close, lasting bonds with one person. Just one. That's what I wanted in a human being. . . . Men don't live as long as women but are luckier when they truly love their spouse because they usually go first. With a man and a dog, the dog will go first. But like someone once said, better to have loved and lost than never to have loved at all.

— STEPHEN ROBERTS, London casting director

It's too true that you have to learn to laugh through the tears. Especially when you're an actor and worst, in comedy. Harry MacAfee was getting too old to be tranquilized for air travel, so he couldn't be with me anymore when I had to fly to a new gig. Climbing stairs became too much for him, so I sold my four-story house and bought a one-level home. I was increasingly in demand yet I knew the heartbreak of having to leave Harry behind while I was away working. Growing old was hurting Harry, literally . . . so eventually he had to be put to sleep. My greatest pal was gone. He was all I wanted in the partner I never had.

— PAUL LYNDE, actor and comedian

Everyone in Japan knows the story of Hachiko. He was an Akita who is the symbol of devotion and loyalty that continue beyond death . . . the perfect dog. Hachiko belonged to a professor with whom he walked every morning to the train station. Hachi then went home but always returned to the station to greet the professor when he came back from work, then they walked home together. After the professor died from a sudden stroke, Hachi still returned to the train station. He expected his master to return from work and walk home with him. This continued for years. People took notice . . . it became a national newspaper story, then there were books, programs, movies, and after Hachiko died in 1935 even a statue of him at the train station in Tokyo that is still very famous and much photographed.

—AKIRA KUROSAWA, director

❖ ❖ ❖

I read the story of Hachiko to my grandmother, who knew the story well but was still moved and praised my reading. She added, "That dog was so human." I agreed, yet I thought, *What does that actually mean? How "human" are humans?* We are not using the right word. We need a new word that doesn't assign a very special quality to one species alone, to only our own species.

—YASUNARI KAWABATA, Nobel Prize–winning author

I became a very big fan of Mark Spitz, the handsome swimmer from San Jose, California, who won so many Olympic medals. He was sincerely nice and shy, unlike many athletes. By coincidence, about that time I discovered a breed of Japanese dog called a Spitz. It's fluffy and white with black eyes. It has a black nose and black lips, with pink-lined ears. It is one of the most beautiful dogs you can wish for. And eventually my wish came true.

—LESLIE CHEUNG, singer and actor

🐾　🐾　🐾

Some humans lack much heart. They're indifferent to pets. Okay. Whatever. But cruelty? There are too few laws to protect our companion animals. Pets are almost totally vulnerable, legally. I am so for what the Animal Legal Defense Fund is doing, trying to create a national registry of animal abusers, to give animal shelters and law enforcement a way to keep track of abusers in their area and keep animals out of the hands of such violent criminals. Like the ALDF asks, "Is community service enough for torturing and killing an innocent dog?"

—DREW BARRYMORE, actress

A friend of mine was referring to a friend of his who's not a friend of mine, on account of his terrible habits. Or habit: drugs. . . . He called him "one sick puppy." I asked my friend to please not insult dogs like that. The guy's behavior reflects strictly on him, not on any known canine.

— CHER, singer and actress

❖ ❖ ❖

The only thing I don't like about puppies is puppy fat, and that's not even on a puppy. I once suffered from it. In movies, on the big screen, no less.

— HAYLEY MILLS, former child and teen star

❖ ❖ ❖

I suggest not giving a child their own dog until she or he is a teenager. A family dog is something else. Growing up around an animal helps give a child perspective and compassion, as well as being fun. However, real responsibility comes later, and caring for a dog helps distract your young teen from their own life changes and concerns. Taking the pubescent individual out of himself or herself and providing another life to look after is beneficial in several ways.

—Dr. JOYCE BROTHERS, psychologist

A dog of any size is a large responsibility for its caretaker. It's not so very different from rearing a child. In both cases one should be loving, responsible, firm, and far-sighted. What seems easiest or most pleasant at the moment may not be in your loved one's best interest over the long run, especially if the easy or pleasant way becomes a habit.

— BARBARA WOODHOUSE, dog trainer

My grandfather believed that giving a child a dog was good training for eventually raising a child. Especially for a girl. . . . There are similarities, especially in the beginning.

— LUCILLE BALL, TV supernova

Some people think a pet is there just for their amusement. That's not so. It's a living being. People have a serious responsibility to any living being they bring into their home. Heaven help the dog with an immature or irresponsible owner. Likewise children, also totally dependent on the personalities and traits of their parents.

— TONI COLLETTE, actress (*Muriel's Wedding*)

An abused child can grow older and tell someone. Animals can never tell. That's why it's important to report animal abuse. Not just for the one animal, but for future animals that same person will likely abuse.

— MARIETTE HARTLEY, actress

🐾 🐾 🐾

Whether it's dogfighting or cockfights or eating dogs or torturing a cat or beating a tired horse, as I once saw in Turkey, it's up to those who care to speak up and say this should stop. Sometimes that will shame and stop the miscreant. If not, report the abuse. If it's overseas, withhold your dollars from that particular place and write their ambassador in Washington when you get home. They ought to know. And let's face it: money talks.

— SHIRLEY MACLAINE, actress

🐾 🐾 🐾

The excuse of "It's part of their culture" is no excuse when it comes to ill treatment of women and animals. If much of the world thinks it's all right to maltreat women, dogs, horses, cats, and others, then much of the world is simply wrong.

— GLENDA JACKSON, actress and politician

We need to be aware how often animals are harmed for so-called entertainment and for traditional practices that have no place in modern, civilized society. . . . A jokester friend tried to get at me when he heard about some abuse and said, "I wouldn't treat a dog that way." To me, dogs are practically human. But no animal should be abused, and there are so many worthwhile animal charities out there that need the public's help. Who else is going to help the animals?
— JANE LYNCH, actress and animal activist

Besides boycotting fur and illegal animal products and offending countries, there's only so much we can do to counter animal abuse overseas. But there's plenty one can do inside our country, and the Internet makes it easier. To name just one longstanding and effective group, there's the Doris Day Animal League.
— KEVIN CORCORAN, former Disney child star

In North Korea they have that crackpot dictator with his nuclear weapons. In South Korea eating dogs is still legal, even if most people don't do it. I can think of at least a hundred other nations to visit instead.
—Sir IAN MCKELLEN, actor

One aspect of my animal activism has been my constant reminders . . . for years and years I ended every *The Price Is Right* show with the words, "Help control the pet population. Have your pets spayed or neutered." Then there were the beauty pageants I hosted. When they refused to stop giving away fur coats I took a stand for the animals that suffered horribly in the production of fur coats. That ended my long and lucrative relationships with the pageants but I don't regret it one bit.

—BOB BARKER, game-show host and animal activist

❖   ❖   ❖

Macao, China, has surpassed Las Vegas as the gambling capital of the world, and a very popular "sport" there is Greyhound racing. It's very hard, to say the least, on the dogs, and we're trying to get it banned. It may take years and years, but you have to start some time.

—ELIZABETH KAO, actress and activist

❖   ❖   ❖

I took a friend's dog to Bingo one night and he was the hit of the show. Every time somebody won and walked up to collect their prize, Prince would run up and join them, barking up a storm. I didn't do it again because my friend said it took hours for Prince to calm down afterward. Maybe he caught the gambling bug.

—NANCY WALKER, actress (*Rhoda*)

— ☺ ☺ —

I like to think my dog is sincere and very perceptive. Either that or she's a canine Meryl Streep. When people are happy, she seems happy. When they're sad, she seems sad. It's so convincing . . . it's in her wonderful eyes, also the way her face moves, the expressions, even the tilt of her head. Sometimes she amazes me.

— JAMES GARNER, actor

The most beautiful blue eyes I've seen were on two very different people: Paul Newman and a Siberian Husky, which technically is a dog.

— KAREN ALLEN, actress (*Raiders of the Lost Ark*)

I think this is how dogs first seduce us. Their faces are masterful receptors of our projected care, deepest emotions, and most profound wisdom. They are the rare good listeners in a world of talkers. For 15,000 years they have flattered us with their attention and intrigued us with their separateness. I think dogs are our first invention and if not our first, then perhaps our finest.

— ROBERT OLMSTEAD, novelist

It's easy to go shopping for a puppy and fall in love with two, and be unable to decide between them. So you decide to take both home. Not necessarily a good idea. . . .

— BRENDAN FRASER, actor

❀ ❀ ❀

Before I ever went to the pound for a new dog, I went to a pet shop. It's since closed down. There were three little dogs I liked a lot. I narrowed it down to two. I still couldn't choose. It's not like selecting a toy or outfit. I was fully aware these were living beings. Then the sales clerk suggested I take them both, to keep each other company. That's always a good sales pitch. I still couldn't decide. Then he says if I take both, he'll give me the second for half price. It broke my heart to walk out of that store empty-handed, but that man turned my stomach. He obviously couldn't have cared less that these were living beings.

— SANDY DENNIS, actress

❀ ❀ ❀

Betty White told me about a lady who went to a pet store and got a puppy, took it home, and found it was so sick it could hardly stand. She took it back and was told they'd take care of the puppy, and they gave her another. Next day, she went by the pet store, and in the window was the same dog, for sale. Nothing had been done to help it. The woman took the store to court and won. And the puppy was restored to health. Two happy endings!

— VALERIE BERTINELLI, actress (*Hot in Cleveland*)

Two of my relatives are adept at teaching dogs tricks. I enjoy seeing that, but have no interest in training or teaching my dog. I just want to enjoy it. . . . One of them says people shouldn't get two dogs if they're interested in training and teaching tricks. Apparently it's much easier to train a single dog than one of a pair.

— DOROTHY KILGALLEN, columnist

🐾 🐾 🐾

If you get two litter-mate puppies, they'll have a bond that you and either of them will never share. They'll be more interested in each other than in you. However, if you don't mind that, no worries.

— HUGH JACKMAN, actor

🐾 🐾 🐾

A singleton dog may make many more psychological demands on you than a pair. Dogs are social animals that cannot be set aside when you leave for work, go out in the evening, or just want to live a life. Their situation therefore changes for the better when they find friendship and fun with a second or third canine companion. But know when to stop.

—Dr. ROGER MUGFORD, animal psychologist

I'll tell you who's not a pet lover. Hoarders. They're all about quantity . . . the more, the better. Quality? What's that? They have psychological problems based on insecurity: more is never enough. Why have twelve dogs when you can have fourteen? Why not sixteen? And so forth. Dogs or cats, birds, whatever they collect, that's what it amounts to and mounts up to: my collection. "Aren't I special? All this belongs to me." Sad and pathetic. But sadder for the collected.

— RUE MCCLANAHAN, actress (*Golden Girls*)

* * *

I could write a book . . . [on] the reasons people would come in to buy a puppy. One lady wanted three "funny-looking" dogs so she could name them Larry, Curly, and Moe . . . her husband was a huge Three Stooges fan. When I asked her what breed, she said she didn't know, just so long as they were "funny-looking." One man wanted to know what a Maltese looked like, because he wanted one to go with the Maltese cross he always wore around his neck. And one man, about forty or forty going on eight returned a puppy he'd bought the week before. The reason? His little son was disappointed that the dog didn't have "super-powers." That's three. Out of dozens. . . .

— SALLY ZABLER, former pet shop owner

Ronald Reagan and I were both involved with the Screen Actors Guild. I was for actors' rights, he was for the rights of corporations. Regardless . . . one time during a coffee break the topic was pets. I asked Ron if he preferred dogs or cats, and his answer was, I'm quoting, "Well, I prefer horses. You can't ride a dog."

—RUSSELL JOHNSON (the Professor on *Gilligan's Island*)

When people grow fond of a particular breed they sometimes think to get a second one of the same breed as a perfect companion to the first. Wrong-o! Dogs of different breeds are more compatible. It's not dissimilar to sibling rivalry within one family. Differing dogs don't compete the same way and are less likely to fight together.

—SEAN CONNERY, actor

Naturally you have to think twice before pairing a dog that's way bigger than another one. But don't rule it out. If the bigger dog is easygoing, mild mannered, sweet natured, there shouldn't be a problem. You'd be surprised how often a big dog defers to a little one. But nor do you want to introduce a little tyrant into another dog's home. It's entirely about personality.

—AVRIL A. FINCH, dog trainer

Just as it's smart to check out a new car and take it for a spin around the block, likewise with a new dog. For instance, does it walk nicely on the leash or pull? Is it friendly or fearful toward strangers? How does it react to other dogs? Toward children? Does it mind close handling? Grooming? Tethering? How does the dog act in a moving car? Is it obedient or does it seem contrary or resentful? How does it respond to commands? To its name? Does it hold eye contact with you? Does it seem to like making eye contact with you? I keep a list, you see. This is part of it.

— RUTH RENDELL, novelist

🐾   🐾   🐾

You have to keep an eye out for your new dog, and keep a protective eye on it the rest of its life. And whether or not it's a sociable animal, you must not allow your dog to bully or be bullied.

— TINA TURNER, singer and survivor

No details, but I learned the hard way not to store sundry items like pesticides, human medications, air fresheners, hair dye, cleaning products, batteries, matches, weed killer, etc., beneath the sink. If you have a dog in the house, store all of these and more in a cupboard high above Fido's reach. Your dog is like a toddler, just as curious but more mobile.

— BARBARA BILLINGSLEY, actress (*Leave It to Beaver*)

If you want a deeper, abiding relationship with your dog you must practice canine monogamy. In other words, one owner, one dog. No other dog. The dog then knows he or she has you to himself, and the bond becomes that much stronger. But that makes the dog more like your child or a partner than a mere pet. The dog gives you more but it expects more. It's a committed relationship.

— JAMES GARNER, actor

Boy, if you want a close pal, get a German Shepherd. They're known to forge a close bond with just one person. I'm sure that's very nice and mutual, but it's a bit too intense and needy for me.

— OWEN WILSON, actor

It was like something out of a melodrama. There I was, a teenager all set for a dancing career, and one day the car I was in got hit by a train . . . my leg was shattered. So much for dancing. A long convalescence, and then a broken leg . . . over a year recuperating from all this, during which time I sang along with the radio and my mother discovered I had a vocal talent. What really got me through all the pain, boredom, and the disillusionment was my little black-and-tan dog Tiny. That was really the start of my love affair with dogs. . . . One day we went for a walk. I was still on crutches, and because I wasn't holding a leash, Tiny ran out into traffic and was killed. . . . It's still very difficult to talk about, and it was my fault.

—DORIS DAY, singer turned movie star

🐾 🐾 🐾

She had some horrible husbands, but . . . that's the only time I saw Doris cry. Her personal life she could put on the back shelf and handle it in her own internal way. But if an animal was abused, it was intolerable.

—JACKIE JOSEPH, costar on *The Doris Day Show*

🐾 🐾 🐾

If you love dogs, try and marry into a family that includes a veterinarian.

—LINDA GRAY, actress (*Dallas*)

Most puppies are adopted at eight weeks of age. By then, two-thirds of the most critical socialization period is behind them. You still have five weeks left. If the puppy sees only family for the first months of its life, it will develop a fear of strangers. Invite different people into your home each week of the first three months of your puppy's life, and have children over to play. What matters is that the puppy is gently held, fed, and played with by as many new people as possible. Save food from your puppy's meals so that visitors can feed your puppy by hand. This helps reinforce the idea that new people are wonderful.

—IAN DUNBAR, veterinarian and author of *How to Teach a New Dog Old Tricks*

I read that dogs bite boys more often than girls. At first I assumed dogs don't like boys as much. That made no sense. Dogs are equal-opportunity likers. Then I read what I might have guessed, that boys are more aggressive and apt to tease or scare dogs.

—MATTHEW BRODERICK, actor

It's important for a puppy to learn "bite inhibition." It's about dogs using their teeth properly. An inhibited bite, a nip, really won't injure a human.

—MICHELLE PFEIFFER, actress

Dental cleanings, done under anesthesia, are also important for our pets. For instance, a dog's gums may recede due to plaque buildup. This leads to pockets in the root line that invite bacterial infections, which leads to tooth loss and other problems, and tooth loss is more serious for dogs than humans.

— EMMETT STANTON, DDS and dog breeder

🐾 🐾 🐾

Brushing a dog's teeth isn't mandatory, but since dogs can't rinse, the nice thing is that they've invented toothpastes made to be swallowed. In flavors doggies like.

— VANESSA WILLIAMS, actress and former Miss America

🐾 🐾 🐾

When I was growing up, my mother tried to trim our dog's nails. Once. She cut too deep, the poor dog bled, and he accidentally scratched my poor mom, drawing blood. Now there's a better way: grinding their nails with a machine made just for dogs. Maybe cats have the same thing, I don't know. But I'm sure it beats using scissors or clippers.

— DICK VAN PATTEN, actor (*Eight Is Enough*)

When our swimming pool was new my father wanted a group photo. So we humans got in the pool and stood behind a small float on which we tried to balance the family dogs and cat. By the time the third photo was taken, one of the animals' claws had punctured the float, so we each had to hold a pet in our arms for the fourth photo.

— WILLIAM BELASCO, agent turned producer

🐾 🐾 🐾

One of the most ridiculous things I ever saw was swimming classes for dogs, held in Beverly Hills. Dogs don't need to be taught! They swim beautifully. Somebody was just making lots of money off of well-meaning but ignorant pet owners.

— ESTHER WILLIAMS, Olympic-medal swimmer turned movie star

🐾 🐾 🐾

If you've wondered why wet dogs wait to shake the water off until they've gotten close to their masters, the reason is endearing rather than annoying. A domestic canine's desire to return to its master's side is temporarily stronger than its wish to shake itself dry.

— BOZE HADLEIGH, author of *Holy Cow!: Doggerel, Catnaps, Scapegoats, Foxtrots and Horse Feathers*

I know a very intelligent music instructor who used to get impatient when his dog sidled up to him, craving attention. Well, what else has a dog got to do? And it liked the man, it liked being with him. I told the man to think of the dog as a small child, because testing has found that the average dog has roughly the intelligence of a three- or four-year-old child. Might not your child come to you in the same way? Wouldn't you be pleased or flattered if it did? Would you get impatient with the child?

— MARNI NIXON, singing voice double for
Audrey Hepburn, Deborah Kerr, and Natalie Wood

I don't think most dogs really like to sit and wait. But yours is willing to do it for you.

— HILLARY CLINTON, politician

Chapter 2

PAMPERED
POOCHES
(THE LAP OF LUXURY)

Times change. They used to call a drab life "a dog's life." But today's canines are a pampered lot. They don't have to hunt for food, they're petted and admired, there's free room and board, walkies, a family veterinarian. In other words, "the life of Riley." Whereas Riley has now probably been laid off.

—HUGH GRANT, actor

My dogs have the run of my house . . . and I have a hotel where dogs are always very welcome.

—DORIS DAY, animal activist

She's my friend, so I didn't make a fuss. But her dogs made an awful mess in the guest room. I'm aware most dogs don't misbehave, but Elizabeth [Taylor] treats her dogs like spoiled children.

—ROCK HUDSON, actor

Dogs are like kids. They'll go as far as you let them. They need boundaries. Discipline is best for everybody.

—ANGELINA JOLIE, actress

Dahling, children are for people who can't have dogs.

—EVA GABOR, actress (*Green Acres*)

I don't like to hurt my dog's feelings. Dogs are very sensitive, they can smell disapproval. When I say no to my dog, I don't say it loud.

—PEGGY CASS, actress (*Auntie Mame*)

A little spoiling now and then doesn't hurt. But I've known of weak owners who let a strong dog take over their lives. It sounds funny. It's not.

—CESAR MILLAN, a.k.a. the Dog Whisperer

I don't think pet dogs are spoiled. Dogs come when they're called. They're glad to be called. But cats . . . they take a message and get back to you. Sometimes. *Cats* are spoiled.

—JUSTIN BIEBER, singer

I had a neighbor who built a lovely dog house for their new pet, only the children didn't want to be apart from the dog at night, so he never got to sleep in his new house.

—VALERIE HARPER, actress

My dad told me in the old days they made the dog sleep outdoors. At first I thought he was kidding.

—TIMOTHY HUTTON, actor, son of actor Jim Hutton

I remember the good old days when dogs knew their place and were satisfied with a bone.

—HOWARD COSELL, sportscaster

My mother and my dog would both relish the opportunity to have all the living room walls painted bone color. Another similarity is that they both have a proprietary attitude toward garbage and its disposal.

—HENRY ALFORD, actor and humorist

I didn't like the idea of my dog sniffing bad things and picking up odors. But I learned the hard way, or we both did, that dogs do not at all take to perfume or cologne. Don't do that to them.

—CAROL VITALE, *Playboy* Playmate

It's not that I hate jewelry. I like some of it. But if I go out and I'm wearing jewelry and my dog's not, I feel guilty and overdressed.

—NICOLE RICHIE, fashion designer

When I splurge on a new outfit I usually get something special for my little dog. It's great when we can be color-coordinated together.

—JAYNE MANSFIELD, sex symbol and
mother of Mariska Hargitay

When I was very young my managers sometimes made me and their dog wear the same color ribbons in our hair. Not little ribbons, either—ones that made your head look like a gift package. I wasn't sure which one of us people thought looked more demented.

—PATTY DUKE, actress

My mother liked people to think we were sisters. She looked young enough to get away with it. Sometimes we'd dress in matching outfits. . . . She got me into modeling, then acting. I put my foot down when she suggested my Poodle and I wear matching coats.

—SANDRA DEE, actress

If you are a dog and your owner suggests that you wear a sweater, suggest that he wear a tail.

—FRAN LEBOWITZ, humorist

My wife once cut up one of my favorite neckties. It was a Hawaiian tie. A fan sent it to me. I think it was a fan. My wife called it my gaudy-awful tie. She used the fabric to make a little hat for the dog . . . and damn, if that mutt didn't get compliments on how he looked in his little goddamn hat.

—RODNEY DANGERFIELD, comedian

When David (Arquette) and I are out with the baby and the dog, we make sure to pay equal attention, so the dog doesn't get jealous.

—COURTNEY COX, actress (*Friends*)

I have to be careful when I get home to kiss my wife before I kiss my eight-year-old black Lab. Franni takes offense if I kiss Kirby first. It's just that sometimes he comes to greet me and she doesn't. Also, Kirby has never been mad at me.

—AL FRANKEN, comedian turned politician

※　※　※

I had a girlfriend I was dating for a while, but I'd never been to her place. Finally I went, and she had this cute little dog with a name that was way too cute. But it really was a cute dog, and almost every time I went to visit, I'd bring him a squeaky toy or something. Instead of buying flowers or candy. Eventually the relationship broke up. It's too bad. I still kind of miss that dog.

—ANTONIO SABATO JR., actor

※　※　※

A cousin of mine had a gay Bulldog, Petey. He was actually gay, and he got a crush on me that eventually became evident whenever I'd go to visit. In a funny way, I was flattered, though he wasn't the handsomest dog. But I was still in the closet, and Petey made me a little uncomfortable. Especially since he was so uncloseted.

—PAUL WINFIELD, actor (*Sounder*)

My nickname is Butch, and one of my sisters' children had a girl dog that my niece named Butch. It had nothing to do with the dog, but anyway. . . . In her later years I met Veronica Lake, who fled show business and was working in a bar. She told me she had a gay cat she called Thomasina. I told her why not call him Thomas or Tom? She just laughed and said she didn't believe in spoiling animals.

—CESAR ROMERO, actor

My husband Fang is cheap and not too bright. Before we met he was given a dog. No cracks, please. . . . She was a black Lab so he called her Black Lab. Fang says he didn't want to spoil her, so he bought her cat food. It's cheaper. The dog liked it but the vet said it's not a good idea—the dog might start meowing. Real loud. Then Fang put Black Lab on a vegetarian diet. The vet was horrified. Dogs are carnivores, they can't go vegetarian. Fang did everything wrong. Long story short: Black Lab and the vet have been together longer than Fang and I—and they make a better-looking couple.

—PHYLLIS DILLER, comedian and actress

Spike, my Yorkie, definitely prefers gourmet. The days are gone when you could just feed your poor dog a bone like Old Mother Hubbard. For some reason, she kept the bones—when she wasn't out of them—in a cupboard. Go figure.

—JOAN RIVERS, comedian and entrepreneur

☙ ☙ ☙

I used to buy my dogs the most expensive dog food. But it's like with human food—more expensive doesn't mean better. Besides, dogs don't always know which kind is more expensive. Sometimes they prefer something cheaper but more to their taste.

—JENNIFER ANISTON, actress (*Friends*)

☙ ☙ ☙

My lil Pomeranian loves to join in, wants a taste of everything I have. I just don't have the heart to deny her. Besides, she pouts if I eat everything on my plate without sharing.

—BUTTERFLY MCQUEEN, actress (*Gone with the Wind*)

If I go to a restaurant and take my dog, I don't expect it to be treated like a pariah. I won't patronize a place like that. Especially when a dog is perfectly clean and well-behaved. And sometimes wears a tiara.

—PARIS HILTON, social butterfly

＊　＊　＊

When I was waitressing I had a coworker, Janet, who had a French Poodle named Fifi. She was so proud of that dog's appearance and its attitude—or *hauteur*. The problem, said Janet, was that Fifi was entering her golden years and she was mellowing. "Sometimes she's still aloof, but sometimes she's childishly enthusiastic." What could I say but, "Janet, remember that half aloof is better than none."

—LILY TOMLIN, comedian and actress

＊　＊　＊

Much of what constitutes good health for people is a varied diet. The wider and more varied, the better, in general. This is not necessarily true for animals. Today's dogs and cats get to sample a wide variety of foods. . . . You shouldn't venture too far from serving them traditional, species-specific, healthy food.

—JOSHUA M. WOLF, pet health columnist

A friend of mine had a neighbor whose parrot died from eating avocado. It's poison to them. So is dark chocolate to small dogs. It's because of a chemical in the chocolate called theobromine—Greek for "food of the gods." An ironic name.
—UMA THURMAN, actress

*　*　*

When that movie came out, *All Dogs Go to Heaven*, I thought what a wonderful inscription for a tombstone. But not for mine—I mean my dog's. It's too general, not individual enough for our own sky-bound furry angel.
—JASON ALEXANDER, actor (*Seinfeld*)

*　*　*

I always say my idea of heaven is a piano, a bottle of fine wine, and several puppies and their mothers listening to me while I sing.
—RACHEL ROBERTS, actress

*　*　*

To cremate or inter, that is the question. For humans, I say cremation. Inhumation isn't morbid for dogs, since they're often sniffing at and in contact with the ground.
—CRAIG FERGUSON, talk-show host

There are two world-famous pet cemeteries, one in Paris and one in Calabasas, near Los Angeles. Famous animals are buried in them and tourists come to visit, so they're not just deserted graveyards. I'm contemplating reserving places for our family dogs.

—DAWN STEEL, head of Columbia Pictures

* * *

I owed some money on a Grecian urn . . . not any old urn, but a future receptacle for Fido's ashes. Planning ahead. . . . It's tastefully done, with beige veins running through the marble, imprinted with a houndstooth pattern—a bit busy, but not loud, unlike dear Fido.

—BETTE MIDLER, actress and singer

* * *

My one dog craved fish, back when fish wasn't so expensive. So she got all she wanted. I wasn't crazy about the smell, but . . . then I heard somebody's cat had choked to death from a fishbone, and if that can happen to a cat . . . so fish was out.

—ROBERT DOWNEY JR., actor

Most dogs have an affinity for some particular "human food." People enjoy telling their friends that they feed their dog, say, peanut butter or carrot cake. In small amounts and on a non-regular basis, most foods aren't harmful. But first, do the research or ask a vet. Make the effort to do both, if you really care about your pooch's well-being.

—REBECCA WATANABE, veterinarian

    🐾   🐾   🐾

We all like to feed our dogs whenever they seem ready to eat, but please don't kill them with kindness. Especially the poor little Dachshund, whose belly is already so close to the floor. A good human companion has to know when to say no.

—EARL HOLLIMAN, actor and cofounder of
Actors and Others for Animals

    🐾   🐾   🐾

It dawned on me that feeding my dogs what the ads called the best brands was maybe a subconscious way to spend less time on their food. Now I take the time and concentrate on giving them a well-balanced, healthy diet, not necessarily a costly one.

—COURTNEY LOVE, singer and actress

Money will buy a pretty good dog but it won't buy the wag in his tail.

—JOSH BILLINGS, humorist and lecturer

Whoever said you can't buy happiness forgot little puppies.

—GENE HILL, author

A dog owns nothing, yet is seldom dissatisfied.

—IRISH PROVERB

Don't be fooled. A little dog may be cheaper to keep, but it's not automatically easier.

—WALT DISNEY, studio chief

I wouldn't be surprised if someone proved that small dogs are aware how cute we think they are. They get used very quickly to being spoiled, and once they're used to it, there's no turning back.

—JAMIE LEE CURTIS, actress and author

Some people complain that Americans over-pamper their pets, like dogs in fancy clothes or the accessories we buy them. Some of which are meant to make life easier or more pleasant for them. So what's to complain about? At least we care about our pets and spend money and time on them. Try traveling to the Third World and see how well animals are *not* treated.

—RENEE VALENTE, casting director turned producer

❖ ❖ ❖

I saw a Great Dane in New York in a Burberry coat and an Hermès scarf. I know I also could be doing something more intelligent with my time (and money), but I'm having fun. What's the harm in that, especially if it makes me happy?

—DANIELLE STEELE, novelist

❖ ❖ ❖

You can judge a society by how it treats dogs. I'm not saying everyone has to love dogs. But nations and cultures that treat dogs badly are invariably the ones that treat women and minorities badly too.

—BOB BARKER, game-show host and animal activist

No abuse or torture or sacrifice of animals is justified by any religion. That's a pathetic and lousy excuse. This isn't an opinion and it isn't "culturally justifiable." Mistreatment of any living being is simply wrong.

—KATHERINE HEIGL, actress

A child's mistreatment of animals often leads to his mistreatment as an adult of his wife and other people. There is often a strong connection there.

—DORIS DAY, movie and TV star turned animal activist

When you don't give a child limits and discipline, that can open up a catastrophic life for him. For a dog, I think it just makes him unruly . . . hopefully you can get the Dog Whisperer to change his habits. Try doing that with a kid who's a spoiled brat!

—DOUG HENNING, magician

One reason I think spoiling my dog is fine and commendable is that unlike a child it won't get to live to be seventy or eighty years old.

—ZACHARY QUINTO, actor (*Star Trek*)

It may vary among dogs, but those I've known know when to stop eating. They don't easily turn into fat porkers—unlike so many human children nowadays. . . . I'm sure animals in general have more discipline than kids today.

—ELIZABETH HURLEY, model turned actress

People getting fat isn't supposed to happen till middle age, and what kind of parents let their child get obese? It's repulsive, physically and morally, and mostly is the parents' fault. What kind of future does such a piggy kid have? Whereas with an overfed dog, well, what other pleasure does he have in life, especially if he's been fixed?

—CHARLIE SHEEN, actor

A child is pampered or spoiled. A pooch is indulged. Thank you.

—CHARLES NELSON REILLY, actor, comedian, and acting coach

There are no spoiled dogs, just ones with attitude. Hey, they're entitled. It's a dog's life.

—JERRY STILLER, actor, comedian, and father of Ben Stiller

I like to see people spoiling their dogs. What I don't like is that dog-kissing noise that every dog lover knows but some people use to excess. That can drive me bats.

   —RICHARD DAWSON, actor (*Family Feud*)

What makes me sad is seeing low-slung canines like a Bulldog or Dachshund waddling along, bravely trying to keep up with their owners, a-huffing and puffing. Not usually from age—from too much food. Which is the next thing to murder on these low-slung doggies.

   —VALERIE HARPER, actress (*Rhoda*)

Don't kill your dog with kindness. Do learn what's good for it to eat and what isn't, and know when to stop feeding it.

   —LIBERACE, pianist

As with children, so with dogs: the word that most benefits them in the long run is "No."

   —REX REED, film critic

The worst is being cheap about taking your dog to the vet. I knew a nincompoop—I'm being very polite here—who any time his dog felt poorly he gave it common pain medicines like aspirin or ibuprofen. Years after he moved away I learned the dog had died prematurely and that such over-the-counter solutions can cause stomach ulcers and liver or kidney damage in pets if not given in the correct dosage.

—PENNY MARSHALL, actress and director

❖ ❖ ❖

I appreciated the fact that when a friend of my parents saw her dog hit by a car she took it immediately to a veterinary. The dog had walked away from the accident, but this kind lady said it was worthwhile to find out whether the animal had suffered anything internally.

—BENEDICT CUMBERBATCH, actor

❖ ❖ ❖

What's good enough for my boys is good enough for my fur baby. She gets the best care money can buy . . . she's worth it and she's grateful. A boy isn't always that grateful.

—JACQUELINE STALLONE,
mother of Sylvester and Frank Stallone

I wish before you picked out a dog and took it home with you that you could know how much attention it's going to need. Dogs vary. Some want almost too much attention. Others are, or they seem, more self-sufficient. Like people.

—MICHAEL RICHARDS, actor (*Seinfeld*)

I wouldn't want to set up house with an emotionally needy or overly dependent mate or pet—dog, I should say. I doubt cats are ever overly dependent.

—DANIEL J. TRAVANTI, actor (*Hill Street Blues*)

People who don't have animals don't know how individual their personalities can be, same as most children. Stereotypes don't necessarily signify. A large dog can be easygoing and tolerant . . . some little dogs are pushy and just have to be king of the hill. Living together in a good fit, getting the numbers and personalities to mesh happily, it's not always easy. But it's worth trying!

—CINDY WILLIAMS, actress (*Laverne and Shirley*)

I do think there are good matches between owners and dogs. Some matches are not as easy and don't work out as well. Dogs who need more attention than their owners have time to give become lonely and depressed or resentful, like people.

—DANIELLE STEELE, novelist

If you're away from your dog for much of the day and your dog gets lonely, seriously consider getting a second dog or a cat to keep your pet company. This is good for your companion animal and for you. It keeps the animal from becoming too focused on you or neurotically jealous of your human friends and relatives.

—NEIL PATRICK HARRIS, actor

I had an actor friend with two dogs, a brother and sister. The brother was dominant, I don't know if it was a gender thing or just individuality. But after he died the sister started to blossom and came into her own . . . she seemed happier than before and was nowhere as passive.

—JOHN TRAVOLTA, actor

They sometimes say if you own a dog you should have two, to keep the first one company. That's truer for kids than for dogs. Sometimes instead of keeping another animal company, one dog or cat inhibits or represses the other. You owe it to your first pet to see how it gets along, if at all, with a second pet in the house.

—K.D. LANG, singer-songwriter

When I adopted a beautiful little Shih Tzu that I named Panda, I already had two male dogs—a little Bichon Frise rescue and a mini black Poodle. I worried that Panda would come in and be intimidated, but the introduction went smoothly—to the point that I could almost hear her say, "All right, boys. There are going to be a few changes in town. I'm now in charge!" And she took over and ran the house until she was sixteen and three-quarters.

—BETTY WHITE, actress and author

In my opinion, three dogs is just the right number. One dog—too focused on the humans. Two dogs—too stable in their relation to one another. Four, five, six dogs—too easy to get lost in the shuffle. Three dogs always have something to do, even if that is only jockeying for position among themselves. Three dogs are never bored. . . . Three dogs is never too many. One dog out of three is always trying to sleep.

—JANE SMILEY, novelist and
owner of twelve horses and three dogs

❖ ❖ ❖

Having an only dog, it would be akin to having an only child. You'd have to wonder if you're doing the right thing. Is one a lonely number for a dog? But is it for a child? A lot depends on the child. How much depends on the dog?

—RENEE ZELLWEGER, actress

What can make a delightfully unexpected difference for your lethargic or bored older dog is bringing in a younger, friskier companion dog. Or cat. This can energize the mature dog and lend a new interest in daily living and playing.

—RICHARD BASEHART, actor and
cofounder of Actors and Others for Animals

I used to think my pets mostly slept while I was away from home. They were always so happy to see me when I came back that somehow I didn't even consider they might be unhappy while I was away. . . . You can find out how your dog or cat behaves and feels in your absence by setting up a camcorder or webcam before you leave. That knowledge can make all the difference to your pet's happiness and to the tranquility of your home.

—JULIE HARRIS, actress

After your dog's been alone for a long time your greetings should naturally be affectionate. But when you leave for work or any long period, act nonchalant or cool. It's harder on a dog when you're extra affectionate before departing—the dog knows or feels imminent abandonment. I was advised, "Cool departures but warm returns for a happier dog."

—JOAN COLLINS, actress

I hated to do it, but it was really for their sake. My Basset Hounds Wilbur and Orville were spoiled . . . we were a chummy little trio, the Three Musketeers. But then my career picked up and I became so busy I couldn't take proper care of them. It broke my heart but I had to give them away to someone with much more time on his hands.

—PAUL LYNDE, actor and comedian

🐾 🐾 🐾

What's happened is dogs in urban situations now relate primarily to one or to two people. In the past, they typically interacted with more people. Also, often, with other animals. Dogs are, after all, social animals . . . pack animals. It isn't that natural for a dog to live with and interact with one sole individual.

—DAVID JASON WEBSTER, veterinarian

🐾 🐾 🐾

I know it's not exactly the same for animals, but when I see a dog—"bitch," if you must—give birth and then, soon afterwards, her puppies are taken from her and each one goes to a separate home, to me that's like breaking up a family. I always wish that the family of dogs and doggies could stay together, just be together.

—MINDY COHN, actress (*The Facts of Life*)

When I lost Mr. Famous [in a traffic accident] it was like losing a member of my family. I could never forget him, and never will. He was the dearest little Yorkie and the very sweetest dog.

—AUDREY HEPBURN, movie star

☙ ☙ ☙

You can talk about pampered pets, and they are. And they should be! But aren't we actually the ones who are pampered? By the pleasure and luxury of their presence.

—TINA FEY, actress and writer

☙ ☙ ☙

If you don't originate from a poor country you are not so aware that in much of the world a child who would love to have a cat or a dog cannot afford it. This takes money. To me, now, I think it is very sad when a child wants a pet but cannot have one. Because of poverty or because of cold or mean parents.

—AMERICA FERRERA, actress (*Ugly Betty*)

A miser or a pinchpenny is an awful thing to happen to a dog. If you're going to get one, you must be prepared to spend as needed. Otherwise, better not to get a pet at all. Greed should be for people who live alone.

—JOHNNY MATHIS, singer

* * *

What goes into those "meaty chunks"? The cheapest ingredient of all—water. Some canned food is more than 80 percent water but is made to look like solid nutrition. The water has been bound up by mostly indigestible gel systems extracted from seaweed, fruits, and tropical beans. These bind water into a stiff jelly which appears as a nutritious gravy wrapped around chunks of meat. In reality they are a device to turn water into money for the manufacturers! They give no benefit to pets or their people.

—Dr. ROGER MUGFORD, animal psychologist and author

A lot of dog food is expanded with air. Dry pellets are puffed up with air to double their volume but not their nutrition. . . . The over-processing in dry dog food can do away with most of its nutritional value. If you care enough about your fur baby you'll investigate the best diet for her. You can't always trust what the label says. Do your own research. Your pet is worth it.

—ELLEN PAGE, actress

I feel that a child or a pet should be spoiled. Up to a point. With attention, not money. I'd contemplate very carefully whether to bring a pet into the house, because it might get enough attention from family members but a pet nowadays is terribly expensive to feed and house and take care of. You're obliged to take care of it for the rest of its life, which can't and shouldn't be said about children.

—DICK CLARK, host of *American Bandstand*

My family was well off. . . . I noticed that people who lived in ritzier houses with fine furniture and glassware and carpets were often more averse to having a pet in the home than people of lesser means . . . I wouldn't say poorer means happier, but they do tend to be less attached to their possessions. Including of course the possessions they don't have.

—VINCENT PRICE, actor

My father was what was called a natty dresser. Most movie stars were, but Daddy took it one step further. He was awfully careful about dogs and cats getting near him . . . he did not want any hairs on his clothes.

—ELIZABETH MONTGOMERY, actress (*Bewitched*), daughter of Robert Montgomery

❖ ❖ ❖

Some people don't have a clue. I remember when Paul Lynde's Harry MacAfee had a growth on his paw that was going to require an operation. Well, Paul was terribly anxious and worried. Another actor who was dining with us advised Paul not to worry so much, since it was "only a dog." Paul threw his napkin down on the floor, got up, walked out of the room, and left the house. And it was his house.

—ALICE GHOSTLEY, actress

❖ ❖ ❖

I read to my dog, who usually prefers fiction. That's because with novels I act out the different characters. I put on a vocal show, so my audience of one reacts more. . . . But we learned an interesting fact the other evening, from a book on animal behavior. After a cow is shocked by an electric wire it avoids the wire. After a dog is shocked by an electric wire it avoids the place where it was shocked. I wish I knew why. Probably they don't know. We can't know everything.

—PENELOPE FITZGERALD, author

I knew that yawning gets more oxygen to the brain. But I didn't know it has "social-psychological significance" till I saw it on a pet show on the telly. It showed how if a person yawns, her dog will often yawn too. It's like a party trick—if you yawn several times in front of your dog, the dog is almost guaranteed to yawn as well. Isn't that sweet? They just want to join in.

—EMILY BLUNT, actress

Dogs are almost infinitely more into scents and smells than we are. So I had the rather daft idea to spray some scent around my new dog's in-house quarters. I almost purchased an atomizer bottle at a department store but rather serendipitously the clerk's father was a vet so she warned me colognes and perfumes only confuse an animal and do it a disservice. So I never did that. As it is, they have to negotiate the world via their sense of smell, so even room deodorants and so-called air fresheners are unwise. Not that they're marvelous for humans either.

—JOANNA LUMLEY, actress (*Absolutely Fabulous*)

If you've grown up around animals, like on a farm, you know that a mother dog circles a bunch of times before getting down to feeding her blind and deaf newborns. That's because she's spreading her scent, letting her babies know where and how far away she is. It also goes back to when a mother dog would tamp down a sleeping area in the wild before lying down.

—ANDY GRIFFITH, actor

❖ ❖ ❖

Scent is one of the ways animals communicate . . . they're very sensitive. They have their own wisdom. Before I leave the house I talk to my dogs—I tell them where I'm going and when I'll return. It's reassurance and good manners and proof of love. What's wrong with that?

—DORIS DAY, animal activist

❖ ❖ ❖

I have friends who, like me, talk to their plants. It's been proven that doing that helps plants thrive. It stands to reason that if it makes plants feel good, talking to your dog or dogs helps them feel good.

—BONNIE FRANKLIN, actress (*One Day at a Time*)

I have a neighbor who dotes on her plants. Fine. Whatever floats your boat. But she spends more time, money, and effort on those damn plants . . . I'd prefer something I can see and hear reacting to me, like a dog or a cat. A bird, even.

—CHRISTOPHER GEORGE, actor (*The Rat Patrol*)

🐾 🐾 🐾

I like the sounds of animals. Birds sing, cats purr . . . dolphins make pleasant sounds too. I love dogs but wish they could broadcast something better than barking.

—PEGGY LEE, singer-songwriter

🐾 🐾 🐾

As a kid, I would try to persuade my dad to get me a dog I could love and cherish, and I'd be totally responsible for it. But no. One time, my hopes soared when I heard him tell my mom and some dinner guests, "I have to see a man about a dog." But all he meant was he was going to the bathroom.

—HUGH BEAUMONT, the father on *Leave It to Beaver*

I was at a meeting, we were all waiting for the main speaker to show up, and someone was going on about an associate who'd been fired and was down at the heels and so on, and he says, "He's really gone to the dogs." I spoke up and corrected him. Going to the dogs, indeed! My dogs, and those of everyone I know, are well-groomed, well-fed, and quite happy to be living in the lap of luxury. Most humans should be so lucky.

—JOAN RIVERS, comedian

Most dogs don't need haircuts, but Poodles need more than haircuts. Styling is required, and it's expensive. And it is worth it. Who wants their Poodle to look like a derelict?

—ANNA MAY WONG, actress

All the brouhaha when the Beatles landed in America and newspaper editorials were condemning their long haircuts. That was nothing new. Irish Water Spaniels have had the same 'do for ages.

—RICHARD HARRIS, actor

I am not kidding. My dog loves to float on her back in the swimming pool. And get a tan at the same time.

—DAVID BOWIE, singer and actor

No, I'm not kidding. Society does penalize the dog. More people are injured or killed each year by horses or cattle than by dogs. But it's "dangerous dogs" that society worries about. We have to keep the dog on a leash. We have to buy a license for a dog, and only for a dog—a sort of tax others don't have to pay. Of all domesticated animals, the dog is the only one subject to penalizing legislation.

—SAM SIMON, cocreator of *The Simpsons*

Don't you think it's like with kids? Those who end up in jail after doing bad things were typically abused as kids or at least unloved and unsupervised. I'm convinced if a dog is showered with love and attention, her personality will be mild and contented and she won't act out and be a bitch. I think only a bitch, male or female, would actually bite if unprovoked.

—KAYE BALLARD, actress and longtime PETA member

That dog [I knew] was treated and fed better than most people I knew at the time. A teacher said because the breed was the Einstein of the dog world. A family friend said because the Border Collie works harder than most men. In point of fact, that was one humble, hard-working, ever-dependable Aussie character.

—PETER FINCH, actor (*Network*)

*   *   *

I feed my dogs filet mignon, dahling. They deserve only the best. I do the same for my husband when he's in a good mood.

—ZSA ZSA GABOR, actress and socialite

*   *   *

Canines' digestive systems are not best served by carb-rich commercial pet foods, but by meat. A human vegetarian is admirable, a canine vegetarian is doomed. Too many carbohydrates cause everything from canine obesity and periodontal disease to diabetes and possibly fatal gaseous distension of the stomach.

—AMELIA WELLS, animal nutritionist

Leonardo da Vinci supposedly suggested that an all-meat diet would make dogs more alert and more aggressive toward intruders. In those days serious robbers typically murdered the householders. Whether the all-meat theory is sound, I don't know. But today's few advocates of a raw-meat diet overlook the widespread risks of bacteria contamination for the dog, the owner, and for other household members.

—DALE LOPEZ MARTINEZ,
psychologist and animal hypnotist

A friend of mine found out that sugarless chewing gum can be harmful to dogs and cats. Now, why a dog would even chew gum . . . I'm not sure they can. But the dog in question experienced a dangerous drop in her glucose level and had a seizure. Fortunately she survived. Now even my friend doesn't chew sugarless gum, though we learned that the danger to pets is from their not being able to process certain artificial sweeteners.

—SHIRLEY BASSEY, singer

You owe it to your dog to bone up—that just came out, excuse me—on what foods are bad for him. Not just foods. Caffeine can overstimulate the heart. Onions, garlic, and such can harm a dog's red blood cells. And so it goes, and so on.

—WALTER CRONKITE, newscaster

Chocolate is simply and undeniably not good for dogs—
and not that good for humans. The pity of it is that most
chocolate ingested by dogs isn't of their own volition, it's
given to them by humans who think since they love it, dogs
should love it too.

—HONOR BLACKMAN, actress (*Goldfinger*)

About half of all canine food-poisoning cases involve
chocolate.

—BARBARA WOODHOUSE, dog trainer

There are many toxic substances that aren't well known to
dog owners. For example, don't let your dog have significant
amounts of raisins or grapes, chocolate, onions, garlic, or
candies or baked items.

—STEVEN HANSEN, veterinary toxicologist

One thing people do too rashly is suddenly notice their dog is
overweight, then suddenly cut the dog's calorie intake by too
much. It shouldn't be cut by more than twenty-five percent.
Common sense, which is not common, says that the weight
gain was gradual, so the weight loss has to be gradual too.
That's how health works.

—BEVERLY SILLS, opera singer

If you're feeding your dog a commercial diet for 90 percent of its calories, then instead of buying commercial treats, use that other 10 percent to offer fruits and vegetables, such as cucumber or apples, and even lean meats. This lets you dole out "people food" treats with very few calories.

—CAILIN HEINZE, professor of nutrition and veterinary nutritionist

* * *

We were in Germany, where McDonald's carried a popular selection called McRib. Years later, someone asked if I knew what Dogrib—also one word—was. I said, "I hope not!" I thought maybe the Chinese—there is actually an annual dog-eating festival in China—or the Koreans had cooked up something new. Happily, Dogrib is a Native American tribe, located north of the continental US. Dogrib is also the name of their language, because their creation story says the tribe's original ancestor was a dog. That's kind of a nice myth, don't you think?

—LEONARD NIMOY, a.k.a Mr. Spock

I had no choice but to become an activist. I've traveled several times to East Asia and have over three hundred videos and five thousand photos, most on my iPhone. I go there to rescue as many dogs as I can. I pretend to be a dog-meat buyer. . . . Some ten thousand dogs each year are tortured, killed, and eaten at various festivals there. A primitive and erroneous local belief is that dogs are tastier if given an adrenaline surge before they die. This is done in slaughterhouses where dogs are tortured for up to forty hours before finally being killed. All of this is on record.

—MARC CHING, whose holistic foods and retail store in Sherman Oaks, California, is called the Petstaurant

❖　❖　❖

Soi Dog was the first organization to expose dog-meat festivals to the West. John and Gill Dalley, its very active founders, work in Thailand rescuing dogs and trying to get the government to enact legislation against this wicked practice. Soi Dog is registered in several Western countries.

—VALARIE IANNIELLO, codirector of the Animal Hope and Wellness Foundation

One of our mottos is "Don't breed or buy while homeless animals die." Instead of adding to the dog population, please remember those who are already here and need a loving home.

—LORI GOLDEN, publisher and editor of
The Pet Press

❧　❧　❧

I am proud to say that Spay Day USA was started by an actress, Doris Day. Although I am from Spain, I think that Spay Day USA should be an international holiday, it is so humanitarian.

—PENELOPE CRUZ, actress

❧　❧　❧

Naturally, people are concerned with and wrapped up with—sometimes literally!—their dogs. But it's good now and then to look out at the wider world and lend a hand or a few bucks to organizations that help dogs, cats, and other animals that desperately need help. Sometimes it's even a matter of life or death for them.

—BILL MAHER, comedian and host

Some people consider giving their pet supplements, but if you're providing a complete and balanced diet, there's no reason for supplements unless your dog has specific medical needs. Even then, you'll want to work with your vet to make sure you're not overloading your dog's intake of a certain nutrient.

—JULIE CHURCHILL, professor of nutrition and DVM

*   *   *

What's so important, not just with older dogs, is discerning when your pet is in pain. Some dogs withdraw into themselves and cease communicating. Some give outward indications like crying or regular panting or becoming aggressive. Others won't eat or lie down, some withhold or protect a part of their body that hurts. Dogs can't tell us when they hurt, so we have to become more sensitive to them.

—MARY TYLER MOORE, actress and animal activist

*   *   *

When you take your dog to the vet or, heaven forbid, the emergency clinic, be calm. Don't panic, don't act worried or babble. Dogs pick up on your emotions. For your dog's sake, keep cool and collected.

—EDWARD JAMES OLMOS, actor

Dogs are more sensitive and perceptive than one imagines. One instance is when you're walking your dog and another dog comes nearer and nearer. Your dog will be strongly influenced by your own body language, by what you do and say. You are, perforce, an example and role model to your dog.

—EDDIE REDMAYNE, actor

If you act or seem fearful of another dog, that's a signifier to your pooch that you're in jeopardy from that dog. This provides a significant incentive for your dog to start a fight. More fights seem to begin with dogs belonging to women than men . . . an owner's confidence level is germane to what follows or does not follow.

—KEN FERGUSON, magazine editor and dog breeder

A dog's self-confidence and compatibility with other dogs derives from the first few months of her life, when she has to be socialized properly. You need to learn what to do and get the puppy as soon as she's ready to leave her mum. Obviously, you can adopt an older dog, which is wonderful too. Hopefully the dog hasn't had an abusive or neglectful early upbringing. It's up to you to inquire. If no information is available, study the dog—if possible try it in a few situations. The chances are it's fine. If it was maltreated, you have a lovely opportunity to make up for it with extra love and care.

—LYNN REDGRAVE, actress

Think of it: a puppy, when it first enters your home, has had the company of his mother and siblings. Now he is alone with a stranger. The stranger decides their future. He may advocate tough love and banish puppy from the bedroom at night and let puppy cry himself to sleep. Or he may have a heart and practice a wise compromise: a box next to the bed for near-contact. Or no compromise—let puppy sleep on the bed, only being careful not to crush him. One will have a happier dog and a happier relationship if kindness is practiced from the start. A good beginning makes for a good ending.

—Sri JEFF OBERHAUSEN,
American Buddhist priest

❀   ❀   ❀

Jessie is a sweet mix of Golden Retriever and Chow. She was no puppy when I adopted her, but my brother Kent had found her in a shelter. They'd kept her longer than usual because she was such a great dog, but a little longer and they'd have euthanized her. Now I take a pocket full of treats with me on our walk. When we meet a dog and Jessie behaves, she gets a treat. Occasionally, when she doesn't behave herself, she'll look up for the treat and I'll say, "No." She's bright enough to figure this all out.

—BOB BARKER, game-show host and
animal activist

When you see a dog tethered outside a store or supermarket, that isn't the time to try and pet it. Even if he seems calm. In that situation, many dogs feel vulnerable or abandoned, so their reaction to strange humans who come along and get close to them is very unpredictable. Try to curb your enthusiasm.

—LARRY DAVID, comedian (*Curb Your Enthusiasm*)

We humans are wont to think exercise is something one needs to prepare for or dress up for. Or perform in a particular place. Or even pay to do. Look at dogs. They're always ready to exercise, to run, jump, romp, whatever and wherever. If we were as ready to exercise as our dogs are, how much healthier we'd all be.

—ROGER MOORE, former James Bond

Who can explain it, but Bulldogs seem to be drawn to and fond of wheels . . . toys with wheels, being wheeled around, and even skateboards. There are some very proficient skateboarding Bulldogs. Wouldn't that be interesting to film? Or to make a film or movie about?

—LANCE LOUD, writer and TV personality

I had a cat who would flee at the sound of a vacuum cleaner. I don't like it either. Later, I had a dog who came running at the sound of a vacuum cleaner. She always seemed to be trying to figure out what or who was inside that noisy tube or nozzle. Pets are so funny, and such fun.

—RON PALILLO, actor (*Welcome Back, Kotter*)

* * *

Dogs choose to stay around people as our friends, guardians, and entertainers. The good thing about dogs is that they don't accumulate gadgets, drive cars, or generally destroy the planet. . . . Dogs are privileged because we can prevent them from suffering in old age by deciding to end their lives.

—Dr. ROGER MUGFORD, dog trainer and author

* * *

Some dogs are natural-born comedians. There's two kinds. Dogs who don't know they're funny and dogs who do. I swear, some dogs do something, then realize it's funny, and look at you sheepishly, waiting for your confirmation that it was funny. Some dogs do have a sense of humor.

—JIMMY DURANTE, comedian and actor

I love how dogs live in the moment. When they play, it's all play. Or watch how they enjoy the sun's rays on them . . . or an un-self-conscious belly rub from their favorite human. Dogs know how to just give in and pamper themselves.

—RITA RUDNER, comedian and writer

People who don't like animals generally aren't very fond of people either.

—REGINE, nightclub owner and former "Queen of Disco"

Chapter 3

A UNIVERSAL
TONGUE
(DOGS ON THE SCREEN)

I loved Lassie, growing up. I wanted to have my own Lassie. But I knew what people would say: "Here comes Mel and Collie."

— MEL TILLIS, country singer

        ❖   ❖   ❖

When I get asked who was my favorite leading lady, I have to say my good friend Elizabeth Taylor. You see, Lassie was played by a fellow.

— RODDY McDOWALL, former child star

        ❖   ❖   ❖

When you watch movies about things or people and places you don't know, you assume what's on the screen is reality. A classmate was saving up to buy a Collie dog, and I'd get to play with it too, some. Finally came the day, I went over to her house, and . . . from movies and TV I didn't know that not all Collies are long-hairs. Her Collie looked nothing like Lassie! I was so disappointed. To me, it was just a big old bald-looking dog.

— JEROME LAWRENCE, playwright (*Inherit the Wind*)

        ❖   ❖   ❖

Lassie has superseded him, but if I had to choose a favorite movie dog, I'm old enough to remember Rin Tin Tin. The biggest movie star in the world at one time. Of course I was a wee lad then.

— Sir RALPH RICHARDSON, actor

In fact it was my studio [Warner Bros.] that brought talkies to the screen, late in the 1920s. Before that, Warners was probably best known as the studio behind a German Shepherd they named Rin Tin Tin. He starred in a whole series of pictures, every one of them a gold mine.

—JOE E. BROWN, comic star (*Some Like It Hot*)

🐾 🐾 🐾

Rin Tin Tin was what is nowadays called a "superstar." Very good actor, though. Dependable. But once we brought sound in you had different languages being spoken, so you could no longer have such a global phenomenon. A dog might speak a universal tongue, but the people around him would have to stick to one or another language.

—JACK L. WARNER, studio chief

🐾 🐾 🐾

We flatter ourselves by saying "humane." But during World War I when we were fighting the beastly Germans, many Englishmen took against German Shepherds and Dachshunds. There were many cases of people killing the latter—small little dogs, defenseless and innocent—because the breed was German-originated. I ask you: What other species but humans would ever be that illogical and inhumane?

—DIANA DORS, actress

I loved that TV show [*Petticoat Junction*]. I also liked that little dog on it that chased after the Cannonball [train]. Years later it was like déjà vu when I saw those Benji films. Then I found out it was the exact same dog! I'm great at remembering dogs' faces.

—ROSIE O'DONNELL, actress and host

🐾 🐾 🐾

There's bad news every day in the papers and on the Internet. But this makes me real sad. At least the Chihuahua that starred in the Taco Bell commercials lived to 15 years, which is really old for any dog, big or little.

—PARIS HILTON, actress and socialite

🐾 🐾 🐾

The Taco Bell Chihuahua ads were among the most charming I'd seen. When several people—apparently several, or else very noisy people—protested the ads because of the dog speaking a few words of Spanish I was flabbergasted by their dismal, biased attitude. What did they expect a dog from Mexico to speak, French? Or do they prefer animals and people who speak only one language, and that one not always well?

—JACQUELINE BISSET, actress

Does anyone remember Laika? The first dog in space. The Russians sent him [actually her] up, in 1957. Of course I didn't like Russia's government, and I still don't, but Laika was a hero. Such a brave dog, helping to expand the boundaries of science . . . going where no dog had gone before. I did consider writing a screenplay about a dog and his man in space. Not that it would have sold. Not if the guy was a Russian.

—CARL REINER, actor and writer
(creator of *The Dick Van Dyke Show*)

☙ ☙ ☙

The Soviet Russians told the world that Laika, the first living being to orbit the earth, survived Sputnik 2 until day six, when the oxygen ran out and she was mercifully euthanized. In fact Laika was on a one-way trip and she died within hours of takeoff, from overheating. The truth didn't come out until 2002.

—SIMONE RUBENFELD, French historian

When I did *Dr. Dolittle* I briefly studied sounds of assorted languages. This was in order to get away from the habitual sounds of English when I acted talking with animals. The doctor allegedly spoke dozens of animal tongues . . . naturally I talked my way through one peculiarly memorable song called "Talk to the Animals." Which you could have knocked me over with a feather when it won the Academy Award for Best Song.

—REX HARRISON, actor

※　※　※

They came to me and said they wanted me to play Dr. Dolittle. Someone told me that was one big turkey and a musical. I told 'em I don't sing and I'm not gonna play some English doctor. . . . It worked out okay. He was more like a vet and he liked dogs and cats and acted like someone you might meet in real life instead of Hollywood.

—EDDIE MURPHY, actor, on the remake

※　※　※

When people find out I'm a professional fish mimic they erroneously assume I must prefer fish. *No.* I'm quite as fond of dogs as the next Englishman.

—RICHARD HAYDN, actor
(Uncle Max in *The Sound of Music*)

— 🦴 —

I always kind of liked movies where a dog or a horse turns into a man, or the other way around. And those Francis-the-talking-mule pictures . . . I guess the strangest project I ever took on was as a fish, a cartoon fish with glasses. It wasn't all animated, but I was a cartoon in part of it: *The Incredible Mr. Limpet.*

—Don Knotts (*The Andy Griffith Show*)

* * *

It's a myth about dogs and cats not getting along, and the biggest perpetrator of that is cartoons. In cartoons the dog and the cat always fight. But cats and dogs are not natural enemies, and there are many happy households that include both a dog and a cat.

—Cesar Millan, a.k.a. the Dog Whisperer

* * *

I always wondered what a huckleberry was. Never ate one that I know of. I know I once saw a cartoon show with a blue dog called *Huckleberry Hound*. And in "Moon River," the song from *Breakfast at Tiffany's*, there's something about "my huckleberry friend." Hmm.

—Larry Hagman, actor (*Dallas*)

I loved Elvis. Loved his music, all the songs. But not the movies—those were the Colonel's [his manager's] fault. . . . The one song I couldn't puzzle out was "You Ain't Nothin' But a Hound Dog." What was he trying to tell that poor girl? It was so catchy and popular that nobody bothered explaining it!

—JULIE LONDON, singer

🐾　🐾　🐾

A relative once dragged me along to see an awful movie called *Old Yeller*. I asked if it meant the dog was yellow or he yelled and was old? "Be quiet. Watch the movie, you'll see." I didn't see, and I hate movies where a boy grows up and now that supposedly he's a man he has to give up his pet like the deer in *The Yearling* and shoot it—if I remember correctly—and like he does in *Old Yeller*. I wouldn't take a kid of mine to see any movie like that.

—MICHAEL MCDOWELL, screenwriter (*Beetlejuice*)

🐾　🐾　🐾

I was in umpteen teen-type youth movies and beach-blanket ones, but the one most people remember is *Old Yeller*. . . . A few people have told me it traumatized them. It was pretty grim. It was a Disney flick about a boy and his dog but that's a real misleading description, though it's true.

—TOMMY KIRK, former Disney star

Such a crush I had on Tommy Kirk! In my favorite film of his he turned into a big dog (*The Shaggy Dog*). I love big dogs 'cause there's more to hug, and I loved Tommy Kirk, and I was so pissed off when they didn't even nominate him for an Oscar.

—CONNIE NORMAN, radio host and journalist

❖ ❖ ❖

It's un-American not to love dogs, right? But some people go too far. . . . On a TV talk show, the way this one actor was going on about his dog, you'd think he'd married it. Then he says, very solemn, "You realize that 'dog' is 'God' spelled backwards." As if this is really significant information. Besides, that's only in English. In French "dog" is "chien," which spelled backwards is "neihc."

—ROBERT CLARY, actor (*Hogan's Heroes*)

❖ ❖ ❖

Our magazine's motto is "Dog is my co-pilot," and we try to live up to that. It's a noble sentiment.

—CAMERON WOO, cofounder of *The Bark* magazine

❖ ❖ ❖

With a last name like mine, it's lucky I happen to love dogs. All shapes and sizes. If it barks, I'm for it. I'm also for that breed that doesn't bark—the Basenji.

—BOB BARKER, game-show host and animal activist

In the media they show the same dozen or so kinds of dog over and over. There's such a variety of breeds that you never get to see in filmed entertainment. Lack of imagination or . . . what? The one kind I understand them leaving out, though I'd personally enjoy *seeing* it, is the non-bark breed, because movies are so about noise nowadays.

—KELLY MCGILLIS, actress (*Top Gun*)

Most game show hosts tried to be actors, then switched. Most are like clones—rather good-looking and rather no personality. My favorite game show host is Bob Barker because he loves animals and he's an animal activist.

—LINDA BLAIR, actress (*The Exorcist*)

There are so many worthwhile charities out there, it's heartrending. The reason I chose animals is they're the only group that cannot speak for itself.

—MARY TYLER MOORE, actress and animal activist

The only time I ever threw my weight around as a star was on location in Morocco [for Alfred Hitchcock's *The Man Who Knew Too Much*]. The locals were treating the animals abominably. So I said until the animals on the set were properly fed and watered, I would be unavailable. It worked. It worked quickly because unfortunately it usually boils down to economics, not human decency.

—DORIS DAY, former actress

There are several cultures in the world and at least one religion that honestly do not give a damn about animals. They believe human beings have the right to abuse animals. That's where I think boycotts should come in. If those people don't understand kindness, they do understand the power of money. Folks, don't be afraid to put your money where your mouth is.

—BETTY WHITE, actress and animal activist

I remember when television wouldn't show footage of one animal killing another, like a lion bringing down a zebra. Now it's commonplace and often it's viewed as suspenseful entertainment, which is appalling. On the other hand, when a news program shows the graphic results of illegal dog- or cock-fighting, that can shock and spur people to action.

—EARL HOLLIMAN, actor (*Police Woman*)

When I find out an actor loves animals, automatically I like that person more. And if they're an animal activist, I'm automatically a fan. When those few people direct their time and lend their name toward helping animals, that proves there's a heart there . . . that's a mensch.

—NATALIE PORTMAN, actress

Movies and other entertainment have a wonderful opportunity to both entertain and educate people about animals. There are movies, including animated ones, often about dogs, that after they're shown in the schools the incidence of animal cruelty drops markedly.

—ANNE HATHAWAY, actress

I saw a very moving Italian film, *Umberto D*, it's on some lists of the all-time top ten. About a retired teacher who's old and poor, so he contemplates suicide. His only friend is his dog Flag, and he tries to take Flag with him—to the other side. . . . The dog absolutely resists, then runs off. To me, that powerfully brought home how suicide is such a human concept, and people shouldn't try and impose it on an animal, no matter how they feel.

—Neil Patrick Harris, actor

I've turned down parts in movies that went on to be successful. One was *As Good as It Gets*. In that movie there was a scene in which a character throws a dog down a laundry chute. When I read it I told the director, James Brooks, "I just can't do that!" I know it's for laughs, but . . . I didn't find it funny. I didn't think it would be a good example to people who might try it in real life. I was hoping Jim would change it. But Jim had fallen in love with the scene and wouldn't change it. So I said, "Sorry, I can't do it. But thank you very much!"

—Betty White, who named her production company Bandy, after her dog Bandit

During set-ups [between scenes] for *Tequila Sunrise*, Mel Gibson and I got to talking . . . somehow the subject became people eating dogs, like they do in parts of eastern Asia. Gibson was okay with it. I reminded him how often some people copy behavior they see in the movies—I asked if he'd do a movie where his character, an American, ate a dog? He just smiled. He didn't say no.

—RAUL JULIA, actor

❖ ❖ ❖

One thing I thought I'd never live down was *White Dog*. It was a film about a dog trained to sniff out and attack black people. I don't think it ever got released in the USA. . . . Like, the things people come up with about animals!

—KRISTY McNICHOL, former actress

❖ ❖ ❖

My mama is an Afghan who looks just like Celine Dion. My sister isn't musical, but she smells like Christina Aguilera.

—TRIUMPH, the Insult Comic Dog

❖ ❖ ❖

People have asked if I named myself after Paris Hilton. Well, if you have to ask. . . . You know, she was the original publicity hound—which I would take as a compliment. With or without a Chihuahua in her bejeweled purse.

—PEREZ HILTON, gossip maven

Movies where animals are made to seem like people don't appeal to me. Contrarily, I enjoy movies where a person temporarily turns into an animal. Those are fun, and the human ends up learning a life lesson from having been an animal for a while. I know I did [in *The Shaggy Dog*]. In those movies, the human almost always turns into one of three animals: a dog, a horse, or a cat.

—TOMMY KIRK, former actor

I recently saw a cartoon movie about dogs where the girl dog was presented as a sexy dumbbell. It was offensive. As if male dogs are smarter than female dogs. Not to mention the act-like-a-slut shtick to please the cartoon guys and make the audience laugh. Haven't we gotten beyond that yet?

—TOTIE FIELDS, comedian

The problem with most animated animal-themed entertainment is the sexism. First, the numbers. Unlike in nature, where every first or second animal is a female, in cartoons and such there's often just one—the token female. Second, she's basically just the hero's girlfriend. Little girls watch this stuff and get the message, consciously or subliminally, that they're less important and are taken less seriously. That in quantity and quality they don't measure "up" to males.

—LILY TOMLIN, actress and feminist

You know how in cartoons and animated movies a female animal character is always distinguishable by her lipstick and long eyelashes and maybe earrings and a bow on her head? What that is, is trivializing and objectifying the female. Making her something like a Christmas tree—something to decorate and hang ornaments on. It reduces her humanity. Just as it would if the same were routinely done to a male.

—GERMAINE GREER, feminist and author of
The Female Eunuch

❖ ❖ ❖

You know how Barbie was the first grown-up type doll? I remember in the '60s when they came up with a grown-up type cartoon series, on Saturday mornings. It was for older kids and teens. *Johnny Quest* . . . about this boy who had neat adventures thanks to his dad, who was a scientist. He had a best boyfriend and this kind of hyper dog. It looked like a small Bulldog. Its name was Bandit and he was white with a black marking like an eye patch. And Bandit got in on all the action. But fortunately he wasn't a talking dog!

—JOHN TRAVOLTA, actor

I have a young relative who is wonderful with [doing] different voices. I myself have done voice work in cartoons, including playing Charlie Chan. I tried to help her, but the field is rather small and extremely competitive. Then too, whenever you have, for instance, a talking dog, most times the voice hired is from an actor, not an actress.

—KEYE LUKE, actor (*Kung Fu*)

Whenever it's a talking dog and there's just one, it's always a man's voice. Every time. Like females are an afterthought. The culture is still so dominated by myth and medieval thinking.

—KATE MCKINNON, actress (*Ghostbusters*, 2016)

I wasn't crazy about how Disney did the lady dog in *Lady and the Tramp*. She came off like what's nowadays called a wimp. But she wasn't my character and it wasn't my movie. I liked the music, though, and the songs that I cowrote. Obviously, so did audiences. Later on, when I had to sue Disney to get my share of the royalties the judgment was $2.3 million. After all, a lady must live.

—PEGGY LEE, singer, composer, and actress

Years ago I was at a party where someone asked if I'd seen the movie *All Dogs Go to Heaven*. I said no but I liked the title. Half-jokingly, I added, "For equal time, they should make a movie called *All Cats Go to Heaven*." This one guy in a red and yellow bowtie shook his head and insisted no, no, cats don't go there, cats belong with "the witches." I stared at him . . . he was serious. A cat-hater! I told him I'm glad he didn't live in the Dark Ages, or he'd probably have been one of those haters who burned so-called witches, and sometimes their cats, at the stake.

—PATTY DUKE, actress

❖ ❖ ❖

I suppose it's the times, but now they try to sensationalize even animals in the movies. Like [Stephen King's] *Cujo*, where a dog terrorizes people. Or cats going on a spree, killing people. But I remember charming movies like *Greyfriars Bobby* . . . about a Skye Terrier in Scotland whose master died and the poor little dog reputedly showed up at his grave every day for fourteen years until it too died. That was memorable and very moving and uplifting. It was based on a true story, not on a desperate writer's morbid imagination.

—ANNA LEE, actress (*General Hospital*)

Alfred, a black French Poodle, was Paul Lynde's final canine companion. When Paul died unexpectedly, Alfred started barking nonstop. He was frightened and confused . . . needless to say alarmed and sad about his inert master. When a friend broke in, worried about Paul, Alfred was still panicked and barking, but apparently relieved that someone had finally come to see to Paul.

—KAYE BALLARD, actress

I guess it's me, and human perversity. When I was a kid working with dogs, I once caught a glimpse of a Chihuahua. It belonged to a lady in a fancy car. So I asked around. A lot. Made myself a pest because I wanted my own Chihuahua. I'd never seen anything like it—like a movable, living toy. But even though it was a success, that breed was still very rare in the US and awfully difficult to obtain. So in time the idea drifted out of my mind. Decades later and then some, one sees Chihuahuas—at least in Los Angeles—on almost any street corner. And it reminds me of when I was a kid and how much I wanted one. But now . . . ? Not really, 'cause everybody has one.

—JACKIE COOPER, child star turned director

When I was a boy horses scared me. Don't know why. Maybe the size. But I thought having a great big dog, like a Mastiff, would be fun, and I could ride it. My mother and stepfather said that was a ridiculous idea, but I was willing to ride it without a saddle. Of course it was just childish whimsy. But one day, as an adult, I was at a movie and I went "*Aha!*" out loud during a party scene where the door opens and in walks the biggest dog you've ever seen. Gigantic! And one female guest gasps and says, "My God, I didn't know horses came that small."

—JACKIE COOGAN (*The Addams Family*),
former child star

🐾   🐾   🐾

One of my library of script ideas was a story from the point of view of a lap dog belonging to the last empress of China. The idea was partly inspired by a children's book called *She Was Nice to Mice*, about a mouse living in the court of Elizabeth I [written by future actress Ally Sheedy]. I didn't go through with it, but if I was going to rework it for today it could be about a lap dog that belongs to a Chinese industrialist who turns into a laptop computer from nine to five—with or without a nine-to-five song.

—CARL REINER, actor and writer
(creator of *The Dick Van Dyke Show*)

When I saw the original *Star Trek* I thought at some point they could have used a pet on board . . . maybe they avoided it because the Russians had a dog in space and they didn't want to copycat or do what the enemy already did. . . . *Lost in Space* had a pet, but it was a robot, so that it could talk and also protect its masters. I think animals in space is very intriguing.

—CHRIS PINE, actor

I like that script, but the boy-and-his-dog theme's been done to death. I'd like to see more about a girl and her dog or a woman and her dog. A woman can really trust her dog. It's just as cinematic a theme as a boy and his dog.

—ELLEN PAGE, actress

Lassie was about a female dog and a boy and his family. I played the mother and as everyone now knows, most or all of the Lassies were *laddies*. I'm surprised no one's thought up a TV series where it's a boy dog and a girl and her family. Though, really, the dog's gender doesn't matter, and the child's shouldn't.

—JUNE LOCKHART, actress

Remember *Air Bud*? I didn't think dogs and basketball could mix. But when it comes to movies, dogs can do just about anything. Money's the bottom line. It's all fantasy. Even Lassie was played by a man dog, and that was long before gender-switching became popular. Maybe they'll finally get real and do a movie or series called *Laddie*.

—JACK NICHOLSON, actor

After *Mr. Ed* [about a talking horse] I was tentatively approached about a show featuring a talking dog. Actually, I wasn't approached—my agent was. He declined on my unknowing behalf. He actually believed he was preventing me from becoming stereotyped. *How?* As a human being with pets? With talking pets? So what? I'll never know what might have been. . . .

—ALAN YOUNG, actor

My brother had *The Dick Van Dyke Show*, and I guested on it and it went over okay, so then some genius decided to give me my own show. It was called *My Mother the Car* and it was a real dog. In fact, it could have used a real dog. One that talked. Why not? The car talked.

—JERRY VAN DYKE, actor and comic

One of my favorite scenes in a comedy is when [in *Poppy*, 1936,] W.C. Fields is out of money. So he takes a dog he's found and walks into a bar and being a ventriloquist he does a voice for the dog that makes the bar owner want to buy the talking dog to bring in customers. Fields pretends he can't possibly sell his little friend, who's so valuable. But finally he gives in and takes the bar owner's money. And just before he walks out of the bar he has the dog say, "Just for that, I'll never speak another word."

—SHIRLEY HEMPHILL, comic and actress

I did not grow up watching many western movies like Americans do. But when I began seeing some of them and the cowboy talked about the "doggie" or sang to "Get Along, Little Dogie," I never saw a dog. I asked someone, who said it was about a calf. Then on the Internet it was pleasant to learn it came from a Spanish word, *dogal*, which is a—you call it—a halter, to keep the calf away from the mother cow while she is being milked.

—ANTONIO BANDERAS, actor

There's a famous story about a director from Europe who was making a Hollywood picture with a popular but untalented star. They filmed take after take . . . finally the director shouted at the actor to learn to "act between the dog's feet." The actor, upset and puzzled, walked off the set. He was later apprised that the director meant he shouldn't just say his lines, he should also act between the pauses. The director had meant to say pawses.

—DOUG MCCLELLAND, film historian

Most movie sequels are boring, blatantly commercial, and unimaginative. I'd like to see something like *Honey, I Shrank the Great Dane!* That would be cute. . . . When you come right down to it, and as some movies have shown, size is the biggest factor in cuteness. If a Chihuahua were, say, the size of a St. Bernard, it wouldn't be cute, it would be alarming. And frighteningly nervous and noisy.

—ROGER EBERT, film critic

When I was very young I saw an eerie movie called *The Devil Doll* where humans and animals were miniaturized. I recall a tiny dog that I completely fell in love with. I longed to own one, and didn't believe adults who said it didn't exist—I believed what I saw on the screen. As an adult I was introduced to small dogs, but I still pined for that teeny little dog. For me, the smaller the better! Which in my case makes sense.

—ZELDA RUBINSTEIN, actress (*Poltergeist*)

Very small canine breeds are often called toy dogs. It's an unfortunate misnomer, for no dog is a toy. Animals aren't toys . . . adults and children should not be encouraged to think that they are.

—MARY TYLER MOORE, actress and animal advocate

One thing I've thought unusual is the manufacture of stuffed animals in the shape of bears for children to cuddle and sleep with. Teddy Bears, Paddington Bear, Winnie the Pooh, etc. Unusual, because bears, as opposed to dogs, are not creatures a child would play with, let alone cuddle or sleep with. And yet . . . I don't think they ever did a stuffed version of Lassie. Maybe it was too difficult to get her furry coat right. Or some copyright problem. But *bears*?

—CLIVE OWEN, actor

                          🐾 🐾 🐾

I was visiting the home of a producer whose husband was a Zen Buddhist priest. I got a tour of their small but beautifully appointed house. In one room, on the corner of a bed, was a lovely and lifelike stuffed dog. A puppy. Stuffed. That's what it looked like. Thank providence I curbed my desire to lift it up by one or both ears to examine it. It was alive. But so pretty and idealized that it looked like a toy.

—DAVID BOWIE, singer and actor

For a time, the most famous dog in America was Daisy, from the *Blondie* movie series. Daisy, the character, was female. . . . In 1939 MGM gave the dog a part in its major motion picture *The Women*, whose publicity heralded the fact that no one in the cast was male, not even among the animals. Then a clever lad discovered Daisy's true sex and MGM was mortified. However, they managed to keep the truth a secret.

—DOUGLAS WHITNEY, film historian

Fala was the First Dog under FDR, who served four terms and died in office. Fala could have been a movie-star dog, he was that personable. Rumor had it that the president wanted to raise and breed Scotties when he retired . . . he wanted to breed for personality, so he could have several Falas.

—SAM SIMON, cocreator of *The Simpsons*
and philanthropist

I grew up with Asta in the Thin Man movies that were so
popular in the 1930s and '40s. Like anyone else, I thought
he was adorable. But I think moviemakers did kids like me
a disservice. Everyday dogs like at home or your neighbors'
just weren't the same. We didn't realize that a dog like Asta
was one in a hundred or one in a thousand, highly intelligent
and trained, with star quality . . . charisma. In fact, rather like
human movie stars.

—TRUMAN CAPOTE, writer

There really was a Nipper, after whom the long-running RCA
mascot was modeled. He was a Fox Terrier who at his master's
funeral was reportedly mesmerized hearing his dead master's
voice on a recording. He stared into the phonograph's horn
with his baffled head tilted. That inspired RCA's logo of the
dog listening to "his master's voice."

—SYLVESTER "PAT" WEAVER, TV executive and
father of Sigourney Weaver

When you think about it, using dogs to sell products is a
natural. Dogs carry all this goodwill that humans have
towards them, and that attaches to some degree to the
product. . . . Dogs are loyal and likeable, and sellers want
you to like their product and become a loyal customer.

—JODIE FOSTER, actress

I remember Sinclair gas stations used to have a dinosaur for a mascot. His name was Dino—of course. I thought that was so cool. I didn't make the connection between dinosaurs and fossil fuels. We had relatives back east who patronized Flying A's gasoline stations because their kids liked the company mascot, who was some sort of a dog [a Basset Hound named Axelrod]. The dog always looked real worried in the ads—because he was worrying about each customer's car. If you can believe that, and a child could.

—DAVID CARRADINE, actor (*Kung Fu*)

My favorite car ornament is the statuette on a Rolls-Royce. She's silver, slim, proud, and elegant. In England we call it a bonnet, not a hood, and we say boot, not trunk. . . . When I was married to Burt Reynolds he had a nameless relative who proudly showed us a Bulldog ornament he'd stolen off a Mack truck. During World War I the trucks were nicknamed Bulldogs because of their shape and durability, then they adopted the Bulldog as a symbol and an ornament on the truck's bonnet. Regardless, I didn't think it was an ornament worth stealing, even if one were so inclined.

—JUDY CARNE, actress (*Rowan & Martin's Laugh-In*)

They name cruisy fast cars after big cats . . . like Jaguar and Cougar. But there's several lean and mean fast dogs—not just Greyhounds—and they don't name cars after them. How come? Also, when something ends up being a dud, it gets called a lemon or a dog. A lemon, okay, but a dog, no!

—MARIO LOPEZ, actor and host

We really are influenced by what we watch on TV or at the movies. Summers in southern California, I would routinely check if a window was rolled down at least part-way when I was out walking and saw a dog in a parked car. If not, I'd leave a stern note under the car's windshield wiper. I was ready to confront the driver-owner if I had to, but thanks to sheer luck I never had to. Friends asked me why I did that—a dumb question—or when I started doing it. I had no real answer to that one until I caught a rerun of a *Doris Day Show* episode I'd seen years before where she did that very same thing, plus confronting the owner. That's what got me started.

—THEADORA VAN RUNKLE, costume designer

The inside of a car can warm up to over fifty degrees Celsius [122 degrees Fahrenheit] in less than ten minutes. Bear that in mind when you think to leave your dog in the car for more than a few minutes.

—Sir JOHN GIELGUD, actor

It just breaks my heart that these films I was in, especially *That Touch of Mink*, are playing, and I want everybody to know that I do not wear furs. . . . Killing an animal to make a coat is a sin. I won't auction the furs. I won't do anything with them. They're in a big storage chest and that's where they're going to stay because I'm so against that.

—DORIS DAY, former #1 box-office movie champ

Societies today operate within different time periods. There are those which still kill and eat animals, even dogs; those which kill and wear animals, and a very few that abstain as far as possible from animal cruelty.

—LEONARDO DICAPRIO, actor and environmentalist

Furriers will protest and rant that that's how they make their living. Too bad! There was a time when some men made their livings as hangmen or operating a guillotine. Not to mention money made from dog-fighting and dog-racing, or rodeos or torturing bears to make them "dance," ad nauseam. Money justifies nothing. Where is the humanity, the sensitivity, of those furriers?

—PAULA POUNDSTONE, comedian

Personally, I'd have been content just to do my comic strip. But I'm thrilled about all the TV specials that bring my characters to life, including Snoopy. They've made Snoopy more three-dimensional, and some children are more sensitive to dogs and their proper care because of that.

—CHARLES M. SCHULZ, *Peanuts* creator

I fell in love with the dog and the bird [in the *Peanuts* comic strip]. I've won numerous awards for bringing all of the wonderful Schulz characters to millions of people who don't necessarily read the funnies. . . . An added benefit has been my friendship with Charles Schulz, who has a dog named Charlie Brown, a sweet dog. He got him from the Daisy Hill Puppy Farm. I once asked Chuck about the possibility of my visiting the place to consider a dog for a niece. Sadly, he answered that the place is now a multi-story parking lot.

—BILL MELENDEZ, animator

My favorite cartoons are the Warner Bros. *Looney Tunes.* They were so creative and unique, and they still have an edge. Bugs Bunny, Daffy Duck. . . . They weren't very big on dogs, though. But neither was Walt Disney. He did include them, but they were dummies, like Goofy and Pluto. He saved the smarts for his mice and ducks. Maybe he didn't much care for dogs. He once said publicly that he loved Mickey Mouse more than his wife or daughters. Imagine being them and having to hear that.

—DICKIE MOORE, former child actor

I vaguely remember, because it's more relevant than ever in today's app age, a comment President [John F.] Kennedy made about education and America's children . . . that they needed to know more about Pluto the planet than about Pluto the cartoon dog. He was very keen on the space program, you know.

—CARL REINER, actor and writer
(creator of *The Dick Van Dyke Show*)

Most people's supposed familiarity with dog breeds is from the movies. But the movies breed stereotypes. Look at Dobermans—simple, friendly, intelligent dogs. In the movies all they are is vicious. Dobermans do have a strong instinct to protect their masters. Nothing wrong with that. What's wrong is people who over-train their guardian instincts . . . and the movies that leave out everything else.

—ANN B. DAVIS, actress (*The Brady Bunch*)

Sometimes a movie teaches you something you don't know you learned until you apply it. As in murder mysteries where the police hold back a piece of information only the killer would know, then the killer talks too much and . . . end of film. A useful tip if your cat or dog goes missing and you publicize it, which can result in dozens of responses, including bogus ones, is to leave out something that only the real finder can know.

—TOM BRADLEY, Los Angeles mayor and former policeman

I did a film loosely based on a former First Lady and her relationship with the Secret Service agent assigned to her. Did I say platonic relationship? The film went nowhere . . . it would probably have done better if it had included a Secret Service dog. I learned something about them during my research for the picture.

—Shirley MacLaine, actress

In view of all the Lassie movies and then the ones about dogs named Benji and Beethoven, I've wondered why no one brings the adventures of Armed Forces dogs to the screen. Such a story could be very timely, set in the Persian Gulf, Iraq, or Afghanistan . . . an action movie, and the dog's handler could have a love interest. I don't get it—unless someone's afraid of offending terrorists, which is not so far-fetched.

—Ben Affleck, actor and director

The entire concept of creating a [TV] mini-series about my life while I'm still alive and without my permission is unspeakably offensive. No one can know what my relationships were like in reality; they'd just shoot salacious, fictional versions. . . . The only ones I would ever sanction for depiction would be my close relationships with animals. And that would have to be a documentary.

—ELIZABETH TAYLOR, movie star

I know movies are mostly fiction, but make it fiction we can relate to. What's with all these humans meeting creatures from outer space? Stick with humans' relations with animals, at least. Dogs, cats, the usual, but don't forget sea creatures— dolphins, whales, seals, etc.

—TONY LA RUSSA, ex–baseball player and
founder of the Animal Rescue Foundation

My favorite movie title of all time? What else? *All Dogs Go to Heaven.*

—GENE SISKEL, movie critic

Chapter 4

DOGS AND CULTURE
(LESSONS FROM CANINES)

Outside of a dog, a book is man's best friend. Inside of a dog, it's too dark to read.

—GROUCHO MARX, comedian, actor, and TV host

      🐾   🐾   🐾

Books improve my mind and dogs improve my mood.

—SANDRA BULLOCK, actress

      🐾   🐾   🐾

Isn't it wonderful how dogs can win friends and influence people without ever reading a book?

—FRED ALLEN, comedian, referencing Napoleon Hill's bestseller *How to Win Friends and Influence People*

      🐾   🐾   🐾

Some guy brought out a book of photos called *Stuff on My Cat*. Like funny hats or whipped cream or any old thing on top of his cat. I'm surprised his cat stood for it. Now I hear he's doing *Stuff on My Dog*. That's not horrible, but it's tacky. So in all fairness, how about *Stuff on My Boyfriend*?

—PAULA POUNDSTONE, comedian

A boy can learn a lot from a dog: obedience, loyalty, and the importance of turning around three times before lying down.

—ROBERT BENCHLEY, humorist and actor

I once knew a Collie who had a search memory for ninety-plus items, so he could be sent to retrieve specific dog toys, *his* rather than *her* shoes, and so on. Unfortunately, our Labrador named Bounce can remember only six such items—his fault or mine?

—Dr. ROGER MUGFORD, animal psychologist

They say the major difference between man and the apes is our opposable thumb. I think the major difference between people and dogs is that dogs can't pivot. They have to bodily complete a circle in order to make a full turn.

—JERRY SEINFELD, comedian and actor

If you think dogs can't count, try putting three dog biscuits in your pocket and then give him only two of them.

—PHIL PASTORET, author

I read that the average dog has the intelligence of a three-year-old human. I find that very hard to believe. Look at all the things a dog can learn and perform. Can a three-year-old kid do that? How do they measure these things? And why?

—WANDA SYKES, comedian

Somehow, a dog can always sense when you're going to give him medicine, and things like that. They just know, and they run off and hide. They're much smarter than little children.

—NICOLE RICHIE, fashion designer

My classical-music education has been somewhat deficient. Till recently, I thought Beethoven was a large movie-star mongrel who got his own sequel.

—DANNY BONADUCE, radio host and ex-actor (*The Partridge Family*)

Dogs can tell music from noise better than most teenagers. Put on a classical piece and the dog is calm and seems to be concentrating. Put on something anti-melody and angry-sounding, like heavy metal, and the dog gets agitated and barks.

—ROSEANNE BARR, comedian and actress

A dog reflects the family life. Who ever saw a frisky dog in a
gloomy family or a sad dog in a happy one? Snarling people
have snarling dogs and dangerous people have dangerous ones.
—Sir ARTHUR CONAN DOYLE, creator of
Sherlock Holmes

In Britain our national mascot is a Bulldog, a proud symbol of
tenaciousness. You Americans don't have a national animal,
but your only two political parties use a donkey and an
elephant—bizarre choices. Especially since American politics
might best be symbolized by a bull.
—JOHN CLEESE, actor (*Fawlty Towers*)

What counts is not necessarily the size of the dog in the fight,
it's the size of the fight in the dog.
—attributed to WINSTON CHURCHILL and
DWIGHT D. EISENHOWER

America is a large friendly dog in a small room. Every time it
wags its tail it knocks over a chair.
—ARNOLD TOYNBEE, historian

The dog is essential to civilization insofar as it mirrors and affirms man's high opinion of himself.

—Dr. MARGARET MEAD, anthropologist

If you treat a dog nicely it'll think you're a grand fellow. If you treat a cat nicely it'll think it's a grand fellow.

—ANDY GRIFFITH, actor

Ever consider what our dogs must think of us? I mean, we come back from a grocery store with the most amazing haul—chicken, pork, half a cow. They must think we're the greatest hunters on earth!

—ANNE TYLER, author

Think how much happier we'd be if, like dogs and cats, we didn't know a thing about death. Think how much more we'd concentrate on the present.

—JENNIFER LOPEZ, actress and singer

A major reason cats figure in religion, both positively and negatively, is the timeless myth that they have nine lives. No one ever said that about dogs. So cats were revered and they were feared. Also, the cat is associated with the feminine principle, so they were more respected in Pagan religions.

—Dr. BETTY BERZON, psychologist

A screenwriter I knew moved to the Southwest and got even weirder. He once told me, "Cats are not heavenly creatures." I said, "*Oh?*" He said there wasn't a single mention of a cat in the Bible. Which may be true, but I don't think dogs come off very well in it either.

—KATHERINE HELMOND, actress (*Who's the Boss?*)

The dog is a gentleman. I hope to go to his heaven, not man's.

—MARK TWAIN, author and humorist

If there are no dogs in heaven, then I want to go where they went.

—WILL ROGERS, humorist

The cat is from hell. . . . Dogs can be heaven-sent companions.
—NAPOLEON, an admitted ailurophobe

❖   ❖   ❖

I care not for a man's religion whose dog and cat are not the better for it.
—ABRAHAM LINCOLN, former president of the United States

❖   ❖   ❖

One reason I favor Buddhism is it accepts science and logic and it respects animal rights. . . . It says not to kick dogs. In much of the world, kicking a dog is considered "fun."
—ELIZABETH ASHLEY, actress

❖   ❖   ❖

The greatness of a nation and its moral progress can be judged by the way its animals are treated.
—MAHATMA GANDHI, Indian saint and activist

❖   ❖   ❖

Hitler said he loved his dog. But when it became clear the Nazis had lost the war, rather than let his dog survive, he killed it.
—BARBARA TUCHMAN, historian

— 🦴 —

Have you ever noticed in those old historic photographs how the humans often look like waxworks and only the dogs looked alive?

—JULIA LOUIS-DREYFUS, actress

🐾 🐾 🐾

To one or other degree, people clench up internally before the camera. . . . In a way, animals are the best photographic subjects.

—ANSEL ADAMS, photographer

🐾 🐾 🐾

Dogs aren't bound by cultural rules and what others think. When they itch, they scratch. A dog reveals its personality pretty quickly. Some people never fully reveal theirs.

—Dr. JOYCE BROTHERS, psychologist

🐾 🐾 🐾

Dogs never bite me. Just humans.

—MARILYN MONROE, blonde icon

The un-self-conscious exuberance of a pet dog which becomes sexually interested in your shin can serve as a lesson for more repressed men and women too embarrassed even to talk about their natural urges.

—Dr. RUTH WESTHEIMER, sexologist and author

❀ ❀ ❀

My dog's recently started sleeping around. Her steady boyfriend is broken-hearted, but she's going through the seven-month itch. That's equivalent to a human's seven-year itch.

—KATHY GRIFFIN, comedian

❀ ❀ ❀

So many marriages break up because one or both partners have to explain or justify. If one simply desires non-sexual companionship, get a dog. They are experts at total acceptance.

—GLENDA JACKSON, British actress and politician

❀ ❀ ❀

The marriage [to Troy Donahue] was very brief. . . . A friend of mine gave us a dog we both liked a lot, so then we shared custody. He got her weekends, I got her weekdays.

—SUZANNE PLESHETTE, actress
(*The Bob Newhart Show*)

Every dog has his day, unless he loses his tail—then he has a weak-end.

—June Carter Cash, singer-songwriter

☙ ☙ ☙

There's an expression: "Every dog has his day." I used to think it was nice for the dog. But when you think about it, it sounds more like a threat. I'm not sure it even refers to a dog—bad men used to be called dogs.

—Tim Burton, director

☙ ☙ ☙

We all root for the underdog, right? We should. But why a dog? Cats get put down a lot more often—I mean grammatically and culturally—than dogs. The word really should be undercat. Except that sounds like the name of a cartoon character.

—Meredith Baxter, actress

☙ ☙ ☙

The first time I heard an American say her dogs were killing her I had no idea what she meant. I didn't think she meant hot dogs, which taste good but aren't good for you. Long story short, of course she meant her feet. Although why dogs came to symbolize feet, I haven't the foggiest.

—Sir Michael Caine, actor

I'm very active, so my dog has to be, too. On weekends we often go camping and fishing or hiking or I spend one day playing tennis and working out and one day exclusively for the dog, running, playing catch or Frisbee, whatever else she likes to do.

—MAGDA NAGY, movie stuntwoman

🐾 🐾 🐾

Most dogs are crazy about tennis balls. The size is right for holding and won't go down their throats . . . the spongy surface picks up and holds scents, including their own for instant identification. Dogs enjoy tennis balls' springy texture; when they chew, the ball squashes down, then pops back up, and it's good exercise for their jaws. For many dogs, a tennis ball is like a child's security blanket.

—MARTINA NAVRATILOVA, tennis champion

🐾 🐾 🐾

Modern dogs still bear the human imprint of having been bred for specific purposes, to advance human culture and interests. For instance, breeds developed for protection are typically indifferent to balls, while those bred for hunting and retrieving, like Terriers and Retrievers, are generally passionate about them.

—JANA MURPHY, dog trainer

Sometimes we forget an animal's name is from human choice. Like, we call it a Chihuahua because that's the northern state in Mexico where the US importer found the dog in the 1800s. Otherwise, we might be calling it a Sonora or a Coahuila or a Baja California.

—CHEECH MARIN, comedian and actor

My dog is named Tabasco not after the place in Mexico or because of my heritage, but from the hot sauce. It was inevitable that my dog be named after a food.

—MARGA GOMEZ, comedian

When my mom and dad were dating in college she fell in love with the school mascot—a big Saint Bernard named Brandy. She even took the dog home with her one weekend. After they married they continued to rescue Saint Bernards. We ended up calling all of them Brandy!

—ROBERT KOVACIK, Los Angeles TV news anchor and
animal activist

Men are a bit more pretentious than women when it comes
to naming dogs . . . Prince, Duke, King, etc. Women prefer
something more true and descriptive, like Fluffy or Sandy. Or
cute, like Chowsie if it's a Chow.

—JENNIFER ANISTON, actress

🐾 🐾 🐾

A friend of mine has a boyfriend who named his dog Tiger.
That's not even in the same species! Either he had delusions
of grandeur or he was a closet cat person.

—CYBILL SHEPHERD, actress

🐾 🐾 🐾

Where does "Fido" come from and what does it mean? It's
such a generic name, it would be demeaning to actually call
your dog Fido.

—JON STEWART, TV host

What people name their pets is very reflective. Of people. Before I married I dated a guy once who used a Roman numeral three in his name, you know, like John Smith III. He wasn't even embarrassed when he told me his German Shepherd's name was, let us say, John Smith Jr. I said to him, "I'd have thought John Smith Jr. would be your future son." Very earnestly he said, "Oh, no, he'll be John Smith IV." I said I dated him *once*. Which rhymes with "dunce."

—DORIS ROBERTS, actress (*Everyone Loves Raymond*)

I'm more comfortable about people who let animals be animals. Without trying to force their individual stamp on them. Sometimes it's a case of trying to create a personality for themselves through their pet dog or cat. Like with the name. Or an outfit. Or a jeweled collar with the name on it. That sort of needless thing.

—JOI LANSING, actress and sex symbol

People in Hollywood often dress strangely. As do dogs, thanks to their owners. On Sunset Boulevard I saw a small dog wearing a pink sweater and a tiara. It was tethered to a storefront, so I never saw the owner. It proves how desperate some people are to project themselves, and they'll use their dogs to do it. If they can't be a pink princess, then golly-gee they shall own a little pink princess! It's similar to American parents who push their extremely young daughters into beauty pageants. It's demented, to say the least.

—HUGH LAURIE, actor (*House*)

   ❀   ❀   ❀

People who put coats and sweaters on dogs usually mean well. People who put skirts or dresses on dogs are rather silly. For that matter, some women who wear particular skirts or dresses look rather silly too.

—BEATRICE ARTHUR, actress (*Golden Girls*)

   ❀   ❀   ❀

Humans don't necessarily stop to think that nature has already endowed a dog, and in fact every animal, with virtually all the coat and insulation it needs. People should keep in mind that dogs are not humans.

—MORGAN FAIRCHILD, actress and animal activist

During winters in London and New York when I see a dog dressed in a coat or a cape I think what nice, considerate owners. But then I'll see dogs wearing the same in Florida or California, where it never gets as cold, and I think, is this sort of a game to these people? Especially if the coat or cape matches what the owner is wearing.

—MELANIE GRIFFITH, actress

❖   ❖   ❖

It's funny in its way. In America people get insulted if you say something negative about their pet. In many cultures, people feel insulted if you compare them to an animal—any animal, even a nice animal. Any animal reference is negative to them. They're that insecure. Here, if you call someone a lucky dog, it's a backhanded compliment. In the Middle East if you call someone any kind of a dog, you're practically asking for a violent response.

—VIC TAYBACK, actor (Mel in *Alice*)

We had an acquaintance in Quebec who owned two ill-tempered Bulldogs. Yet she hated cats. Whenever I hear the word "dogmatic" in English, I think of this lady, who was from Toronto. When I was a kid I thought dogmatic meant someone who hated cats and was stubborn and crabby. Later I found out the word has nothing to do with dogs.

—MICHAEL SARRAZIN, actor

There are some Korean immigrants who come to the US and have never heard of hot dogs, and when they do they're horrified. Others think, "Oh, just like home—they eat dogs." Which not all Koreans do. But you must admit it's a peculiar name for an American food.

—JOHNNY YUNE, Korean American comedian

My favorite foods are French fries and hot dogs and I'm so very proud that Pink's [the famous hot dog stand] named one of their menu items after me. It makes me feel like I'm a real part of Los Angeles culture—which is not an oxymoron, people! They call it the Betty White Naked Dog because I like mine plain, with no condiments.

—BETTY WHITE, actress and former game-show panelist

My background is German, and they invented hot dogs. They brought over the sausage and made it popular here, in a long bun . . . then it became an all-American food. One such food I never cared for is apple pie, which when I first said that publicly it caused a minor uproar. I'm truly pleased to hear that my hometown, Cincinnati, now has an establishment called Paws & Refresh where a dog can get a shampoo and a nail trim.

—DORIS DAY (born Doris von Kappelhoff)

They have an expression in the States: "putting on the dog." I've heard it a few times there. It means acting ostentatious or pretentious. Which has nil to do with dogs and everything to do with humans trying to impress. One wonders how such expressions get started, and why they endure.

—JOHN SCHLESINGER, director

You've heard of hair of the dog? It means an alcoholic drink that one takes to cure a hangover! It comes from another illogical saying, "the hair of the dog that bit you," which was the prescribed remedy when one got bitten by a mad dog. Obviously, olden-days people weren't particularly enlightened. Or practical.

—STEPHEN FRY, actor and author

One of our rescue dogs was because the previous owner became an alcoholic and neglected to feed or walk the dog properly. Of course when that happens, the poor dog can't really communicate it to anybody. The power of speech that animals lack is their great vulnerability. For the most part, they suffer in silence.

—CHARLOTTE RAE, actress (*The Facts of Life*)

Animal-abuse hotlines are one of the best recent inventions, more than most electronic gadgets. In the past that I remember vividly, if somebody abused their own kid most people would say it's none of my business, stay out of it, and if someone abused their own pet most people would say it's only an animal, after all. Thank goodness times have changed.

—MEL BROOKS, comedian, actor, writer, and director

One of the easiest ways to get a federal grant is to perform experiments on animals. . . . Nearly all these experiments yield no new information, just suffering for animals, including cats and dogs. Yet the NIH [National Institutes of Health] keeps the cycle going. Unethical people keep torturing animals just to earn grant money. Many of these tests are redundant— identical tests done over and over at different universities, a complete waste of taxpayer money.

—BOB BARKER, game-show host and animal activist

The cosmetics industry is a major source of barbaric experiments on animals. For example, testing cosmetics on the eyes of dogs and chimpanzees. And intentionally blinding animals in stupid, meaningless tests. . . . When you buy these products, look for a notice that they haven't been tested on animals. If there's no such information, boycott the product and let the manufacturer know why.

—LORETTA SWIT, actress (*M*A*S*H*)

Human beings flatter themselves when they say "humane." Historically, the way humans have treated each other and especially animals has been very far from humane and, indeed, all too human.

—HAROLD WILSON, former prime minister of the United Kingdom

Isn't it great how with dogs they all mix in? They just meet up and do it together, regardless of breed or color or even size. They don't segregate or have laws about who you can't pair off with . . . they don't discriminate. On the other hand, some people might call that promiscuity.

—MARIAH CAREY, singer

I love how a feisty little dog can stand up to a much bigger dog in a way that the average poor man hardly ever can with a rich or important man. With dogs it's more about personality than type.

—CANDICE BERGEN, actress

Human culture is largely about differentiation. "You're different from me, so I'm better than you." Rather than finding the commonality. Animals don't have a class system, that's totally alien to them. . . . And be cognizant that it is humans who choose to elevate one dog breed above another and put someone else's dog down as a mutt, etc. Selfish humans seldom stop seeing, exaggerating, or even creating differences.

—Sir CHRISTOPHER LEE, actor

The culture of democracy declares that all people are created equal. Wrong on both counts. . . . Some people are smarter than others, which is admirable. Some are better-looking, which is not, unless they're older, which implies upkeep. Likewise, some dogs and cats are personable and charming, others aren't. As for differing intelligence levels among pets, of that I claim no knowledge.

—Sir ANTHONY ASQUITH, director

Sadly, some dogs are just dogs. You can get a puppy who looks cute but grows up to have no personality and just turns out to be "a dog," rather than someone special. . . . A close friend had a dog that grew up to be very dull, the way some people turn out to be bores. Not everyone has a great personality, and not all dogs do either.

—Danielle Steele, novelist

Not long ago, walking on a street near my home, I slowed down near a woman whose little dog was doing its business. Our eyes met. Mine and the dog's. I swear, that dog was embarrassed that I was watching it at that moment. Its expression and its barely but perceptibly changed posture absolutely told me my gaze had embarrassed that little fur person. You can't tell me dogs don't have individual personalities.

—Rod McKuen, poet

One afternoon in Kaohsiung, Taiwan, I was taking a walk and saw a middle-aged woman peeing near some shrubs. I was surprised, not quite shocked. It seemed and was quite natural. We tend to be shocked too often by natural things. Looking at animals behave, we're brought back down to earth. Animals are nothing if not natural. Unlike our own species.

—Dong Kingman, artist

A producer friend of mine decided to have a portrait painted of the family dog for his wife's birthday. I saw the result, it was very life-like and the dog was quite beautiful. But it was a male dog, which the painter had made unclear. In real life it was clear. The wife complained, but the painter wouldn't make, uh, any addition or correction. So the couple returned the painting and got half their purchase price back. The painter was adamant. He said he delivered only G-rated portraits.

—BILL ASHER, TV producer (*Bewitched*)

❧   ❧   ❧

He was the love of my life, was Harry MacAfee—same name as the character I played on Broadway in *Bye Bye Birdie* and in the movie. He was a Dandie Dinmont, a rare and special breed . . . I commissioned an oil painting of him. Some folks thought that was a bit much. Shows how little they knew. I could have commented on how some men have paintings done of a wife who no longer remotely resembles the painting, which can't be very pleasant for her. But Harry looked exactly the same way until the day he passed.

—PAUL LYNDE, actor and comedian

I had the cutest little black boy dog, named Samson. Sometimes I was tempted to give him a haircut but on account of the name I was superstitious. Besides, he had lovely, fluffy hair. I didn't want to spoil his looks. It's nice to be able to look at and admire a male without his minding it or necessarily opening his big yap.

—BARBARA NICHOLS, actress

     🐾   🐾   🐾

My daughter was terribly self-conscious about her freckles when she was very young. At one point we were given the opportunity to obtain a purebred Dalmatian puppy for free. I thought it would be a nice companion for Ginger, but she said no, she didn't want a dog that had freckles, and black ones, at that!

—LELA ROGERS, stage mother

When I was a kid I wanted a Dalmatian. This was long before everyone wanted one because of *101 Dalmatians*. I didn't care what it looked like, I liked that it was the fireman's mascot, 'cause in the old days Dalmatians ran ahead of horse-drawn fire engines to clear the way for 'em. The chief at the local fire station never noticed I was a girl until he took me aside one day to ask why I hung around there so much. I said I wanted to be a fireman when I grew up. He told my mother, who was horrified and immediately enrolled me in a dance class. Which didn't change a thing. And I insisted it be tap, 'cause I wouldn't do no ballet in a million years.

—Patsy Kelly, comedic actress

* * *

If you want to talk about unsung heroes, how about dogs in the military that are just as brave as any soldier and perform amazing feats. There've been a few books about them, but they don't usually get much media attention . . . I'd look forward to a movie where Lassie joins the Army.

—Judith Crist, film critic

* * *

I so much admire the dogs that bring out to life the people trapped in fallen buildings from earthquakes, like in Italy this year [2016]. Imagine being able to do that, saving the lives of terrified, almost hopeless people because of their superior senses of smell and hearing. Fabulous!

—Roberto Benigni, actor and director

I wrote a fabulous book about Josephine, my darling black Poodle [*Every Night, Josephine*]. I was flabbergasted it didn't become a bestseller. What were people reading, instead? So I analyzed it and found readers didn't want a lovely book about a darling dog, they wanted something melodramatic about people who didn't behave in lovely ways. That's just what I gave them, with a vengeance!

—JACQUELINE SUSANN, whose *Valley of the Dolls* outsold every novel since *Gone with the Wind*

There are many examples of popular dogs or hero dogs in literature. It is not so easy to find a hero cat or a lovable cat. But there is one, in my next movie: the Puss in Boots.

—ANTONIO BANDERAS, actor

You know the four-eyes thing that dumb kids call someone who wears glasses? I thought if you wore glasses you were smarter than kids who didn't. One reason was the cartoon character Mr. Peabody, who was a dog. He wore glasses and everyone called him Mister. He was self-composed and unemotional, like Mr. Spock, and he was a math genius, like Einstein. He was always solving problems, including those of the human boy who tagged along with him. I thought Mr. Peabody was heroic.

—JASON ALEXANDER, actor (*Seinfeld*)

When I was a kid there was a cartoon series for kids—or is that not redundant any more?—which the name I don't remember. It costarred a dumb, dopey-sounding dog. Even then, I kind of resented it. It was so silly and condescending. The poor dog was the sidekick of a human who usually had to get the dog out of some predicament. I mean, you just knew a human had to have created that series, right?

—JIM CARREY, comedic actor (*Dumb and Dumber*)

I thought the Hound of the Baskervilles was poorly served by [author] Arthur Conan Doyle. He tried to make the dog the villain of the piece, but that was a red herring. The villain was a human. All that made the dog seem villainous was the phosphorescent paint somebody coated him with, so he would glow bright and large in the dark . . . I felt sorry for the hound, whose only flaw, as it were, was being too large to be cuddly.

—JUDE LAW, actor

I realize foxes and wolves are distinct, but they are related. I am for the underdog, and I always root for the fox in those awful fox hunts. That's the reason I recommend the [movie] musical *Mame*, where Lucille Ball rescues the fox. Though of course if the fox were as big as a wolf I doubt we would be as compassionate toward it.

—YOKO ONO, musician

"Red herring," one of my favorite expressions, has nothing whatever to do with bloody fish. Rather, it's due to the reddish-brown color of the smelly herring which 19th-century animal lovers employed to provide a false scent to the dogs of the English aristocracy who were following them on horseback while the dogs chased a fox to its death. These soft-hearted souls dragged the preserved fish along the dogs' route but away from the beleaguered fox. The red herrings were meant to deceive, as in my pictures.

—ALFRED HITCHCOCK, director

Culturally, the wolf has long been demonized, as is sometimes the case with a large or lone dog. There is also the myth that inside every dog lurks a bit of wolf. Untrue. It derives from the assumption that our ancestors tamed or domesticated wolves into dogs. . . . The significant differences between dogs and wolves have recently been proved by intensive study of the canine genome and mitochondrial DNA. It's also been proven that more than two-thirds of modern dog breeds descend from an Asian proto-canis ancestor.

—Dr. HILLARY HUNTER, evolutionary biologist

The ordinary housecat is actually closer to a tiger than a pet dog is to a wolf.

—CAMERON DIAZ, actress

The roar of a big cat like a lion or tiger is pretty scary. A wolf doesn't have a large, wide-ranging roar, it has that eerie howl that in its way is just as scary. . . . If a domestic cat were the size of a tiger, would it still purr or would it roar?

—MATT BOMER, actor

🐾   🐾   🐾

[The wolf's] appearance may fool us into thinking "dog," but its behavior is often not human-friendly. Which can induce a feeling of betrayal. Besides, where a dog is happy to bond with a human and virtually forsake other canines, the wolf is very much a pack animal, therefore more aloof to us and far more intimidating.

—Dr. GIL FERGUSON, British zoologist

🐾   🐾   🐾

The phrase "lone wolf" isn't accurate. Mostly it's used about solitary humans but it applies much more to a dog than to a wolf. It's mostly or only in the movies that a wolf is alone.

—CHARLES MARTIN SMITH, actor
(*Never Cry Wolf*) turned director

— 🦴 —

The big bad wolf symbolizes sexuality and sexual threat. A womanizer is sometimes called a wolf. Often he produces a wolf whistle.... The tales "Little Red Riding Hood" and "The Three Little Pigs" have more than a little to do with devouring and assault and sexual violation. In comparison, the dog's cultural and literary image is virtually sex-free. Unlike the cat's ... as in cat-house, catting about, tomcats, and so forth.

—MARIO PEI, linguist and philologist

That's one saying I don't get. How can a dog's bark be worse than his bite? His bark don't hurt you none.

—MEL TILLIS, country singer

You have to hand it to ad companies when it comes to imagination. I remember ads for Naldecon cough syrup [made by Bristol Laboratories] that used a coughing dog against what they called "barking coughs." I could sometimes identify with that, although I never saw a dog cough. But some ads are cute, where most are boring or irksome. I like ads with animals in them.

—EILEEN HECKART, actress (*Butterflies Are Free*)

I didn't know they spell gray "grey" in England. Anyway, I read in a book that back when the Greyhound bus company had only one bus the owner painted it gray. 'Cause any other color would look dirty after spending hours on a dusty road . . . and I remember when roads weren't all paved! So one day someone tells the owner his bus looks like a gray dog or a Greyhound racing through the country, and that gives the guy the idea for his logo [slogan], "Ride the Greyhound."

—EARL HOLLIMAN, former actor and animal activist

I'm from the South, where catfish were usually served with cornmeal biscuits. Hush puppies came from its deep-fried batter. The story goes that during the deep poverty after the Civil War, mothers would feed their kids some fried corn batter to quiet their crying from hunger. Or to quiet the family dog. And Mama would say, "Hush, child," or "Hush, puppy." I also heard hunters did the same to quiet a noisy mutt with "Hush, dog," or "Hush, puppy."

—FANNIE FLAGG, actress turned author

I remember when the Wolverine shoe company brought out a new kind of shoe in the early '60s. They named them Hush Puppies. Their mascot was a droopy-eyed, droopy-eared dog . . . a Basset Hound. The shoes were soft-soled and the name was about them being quiet and being smooth like a puppy's coat. They were popular shoes, very comfortable.

—ADAM WEST, TV's Batman

To me, puppy love is all about falling in love with dogs and doggies. It's nothing to do with pimply teenagers.

—CHEVY CHASE, actor

I've been called a puppy in my time. We still use it occasionally about a young male who's what you Americans call too big for his britches. Or a youth who deigns to correct his elders. Now, what any of that has to do with baby dogs, I can't fathom.

—COLIN FIRTH, actor

The idea of a dog [Spuds MacKenzie] to advertise Bud Light Beer and legitimize being a lech and a beer guzzler was in totally poor taste. Unsurprisingly, it caught on with the young. Fortunately the backlash made "Spuds" change his tune; he moved ahead to public service announcements warning about drinking and driving.

—JOHN FORSYTHE, actor (*Dynasty*)

🐾 🐾 🐾

What were people so shocked about? So Spuds MacKenzie was enacted by a female dog. Lassie was played by a male dog. Everyone knows that. Don't they? And turnabout is fair play.

—SCOTT CAAN, actor

🐾 🐾 🐾

Do you know that the #1 talk show host in China, with 100 million viewers a day, is transgender? She was born a man. This makes me question why numerous and assorted people in the West are so concerned to find out the gender of a dog. How can it matter to them? Either you like dogs or you don't. In India not everyone likes dogs. Not yet. When they reach the standard of living of the West, that will change. Right now, for many people, dogs are competition for food.

—KUNAL NAYYAR, actor (*The Big Bang Theory*)

The Chinese zodiac has a Year of the Dog. There is no Year of the Cat. One explanation is that China has always emphasized cleanliness, so rats did not proliferate as in Europe, where they caused the Black Death.

—JET LI, action star

❧ ❧ ❧

I am somewhat ashamed that the Chow is a Chinese dog . . . to explain, it is a fine dog, but in Mandarin Chinese "chow" means to cook and in Cantonese Chinese, which we speak in Hong Kong, "chow" means food. Unfortunately, the Chow dog used to be food, so it was called Chow Chow. Buddhism is most animal-friendly, but many Chinese are not Buddhist.

—LESLIE CHEUNG, singer and actor

❧ ❧ ❧

When I heard about dogfish I wanted to see what that looked like. It's a shark! Not a big shark—it has a long tail—but it is a shark.

—PATRICK DUFFY, actor (*Dallas*)

I was rather offended when I watched an episode of a sitcom I otherwise always enjoy, *Fawlty Towers*. I'm partial to Shih Tzus, and in the show a woman had one. She was mock-spanking it when an old man comes by and says oh, dear, oh, dear, and stares at her dog. The lady tells him it's a little Shih Tzu. The old man nods, then asks what breed it is. Well, you get the implication. . . .

—JACKIE COLLINS, novelist

The Canary Islands, which belong to Spain, were not named after the little yellow birds. When the Romans landed there they saw animals in the distance. The Romans thought they were dogs. So they named them the Canariae Insulae—Islands of the Dogs. Then they named the birds on the islands "canaries" after what they thought were dogs. You see, geography can be fun!

—JAVIER BARDEM, actor

Dog days are the hottest part of the year—when a dog gets hot under the collar—reckoned in ancient times from the simultaneous rising of the sun and Sirius, the brightest star in the sky. Sirius is the dog star, which appears to follow on the heels of Orion the hunter.

—BOZE HADLEIGH, author of *Holy Cow!*

A lot of expressions bear no logic, they're just alliterative. People like alliteration. So you have bats in the belfry, but also bulldogs in the belfry. I've used "bulldogs in the belfry" in my writing. Why? I like the sound of it.

—RAY BRADBURY, science fiction author

After I heard someone call her dog a mutt I looked it up. I figured it was short for another word, and it was: muttonhead. But that came from sheep, and long ago a stupid person, being compared to a sheep, was called a muttonhead. That got shortened to mutt and then transferred to mixed-breed dogs because people thought mongrels, or mixed breeds, were less intelligent than a pure breed. So it would be ironic to call a Sheepdog a mutt.

—KEVIN CURRAN, TV writer and producer

One of the worst things to call somebody in Germany, a double insult, is Schweinhund. It means pig-dog.

—VERUSCHKA, German supermodel

They took so many German words and changed the meaning! Now in TV and films they say to "sic" a dog on someone, as if it is an order to attack. But to sic originally meant to find, from the German verb *suchen*, to look for. The trained dog is often a police or tracking dog, and it is not told to attack, it is told to seek and find. But you know how the movies are. . . .

—PAUL HENREID, actor turned director

🐾 🐾 🐾

I don't set the dogs on them, but if I see them approach my house I shout at them through a megaphone. . . . In public if they approach me, I say, "I will sign [an autograph] for you if you sign for me a check to help abused or homeless dogs." Some agree, and that makes me happy—it means they care about me and about life. But most walk away quickly.

—BRIGITTE BARDOT, sex symbol turned animal activist

🐾 🐾 🐾

I don't know what launched and maintains this fan-culture phenomenon of people trying to acquire a celebrity's signature on a piece of paper. No one is able to tell me, and I don't like giving autographs—they're the same thing you sign on your checks. What I don't mind is doing a sketch of Snoopy . . . and then I sign it "Sparky," a nickname I have.

—CHARLES M. SCHULZ, creator of Snoopy

Chapter 5

CUR-MUDGEONS!
(NOT EXACTLY PRO-POOCH!)

Dogs like everybody. Cats are more selective.

—TINA LOUISE, actress (*Gilligan's Island*)

❈ ❈ ❈

Dogs look up to you. Cats look down on you. Give me a pig. He just looks you in the eye and treats you like an equal.

—WINSTON CHURCHILL, former prime minister
of the United Kingdom

❈ ❈ ❈

You can say any foolish thing to a dog and the dog will give you a look that says, "Wow, you're right! I never would've thought of that!"

—DAVE BARRY, author and columnist

❈ ❈ ❈

By what right has the dog come to be regarded as a "noble" animal? The more brutal and cruel and unjust you are to him the more your fawning and adoring slave he becomes. Whereas if you shamefully misuse a cat she will always maintain a dignified reserve toward you afterward—you will never get her full confidence again.

—MARK TWAIN, author and humorist

The noblest of all animals is the dog, and the noblest of all dogs is the hot dog. It feeds the hand that bites it.

—OSCAR MAYER, wiener king

*   *   *

It's sometimes theorized that dogs can actually think. I don't buy it. If they could, they wouldn't think so highly of people.

—JOHNNY DEPP, actor

*   *   *

It's hard to believe, but some people claim their dogs are almost human—and they mean it as a compliment.

—attributed to OSCAR WILDE and NOEL COWARD

*   *   *

Talk about Pavlov's dogs. Lots of male humans are the same when it comes to conditioning. Many dislike cats because they're supposed to. On sexist principle. Like: female cat owner, male dog owner. That sort of man lets society do his thinking for him.

—SUSAN SARANDON, actress and activist

A man who was loved by three hundred women singled me out to live with him. Why? I was the only one without a cat.

—ELAYNE BOOSLER, comedian

I went out with a guy who had a cat. Later, I went out with a guy who had a dog. He explained that he had to walk the dog twice every day and that on weekends and one weekday a week he had to spend lots of time playing with his dog to give it enough exercise. The first guy didn't have to do any of that for his cat. Both were nice guys. I started seeing the first guy again.

—CARRIE HAMILTON, writer and actress, daughter of Carol Burnett

My wife said she didn't want a pet dog. Didn't want any kind of dog in the house. I asked why not? She tries to be sarcastic . . . says she doesn't want a home on the mange, or vice versa.

—RODNEY DANGERFIELD, comedian

Do you ever walk into a room and forget why you walked in? I think that's how dogs spend their lives.

—SUE MURPHY, comedian

A Pekingese spends half his life trying to keep his tongue in his mouth.

—DAN LIEBERT, author and aphorist

You visit someone with a big dog. Big dogs have big, persistent tongues. The owner says, "He likes you." The dog starts humping your leg. The owner says, "He wants to play with you." The big dog tries to land in your lap. The owner says, "He wants to nest there." So I say, "Sorry, gotta fly." I'm more careful who I visit now.

—ROBIN WILLIAMS, actor and comedian

Us humans misperceive things . . . like a dog humping your shin. Maybe he's in love with you? *Not.* Vets say it's mostly about asserting himself, and the longer they do it the more powerful they feel, and that can lead to problems. Who knew, right?

—ADAM SANDLER, actor, writer, and producer

My cats are playful. Sometimes. So am I. Sometimes. But a dog is always ready to retrieve a stick. Why? Just because somebody throws it.

—SANDY DENNIS, actress

I admire the boundless energy of dogs. Whatever their size, they're up to fetching a stick, playing Frisbee, chasing after a bicycle, etc., etc. A shame they never put all that energy to any good use. I wish I had some of that excess energy.

—JONATHAN FRID, actor (Barnabas in *Dark Shadows*)

🐾 🐾 🐾

It's rather jarring when a date shows you one photo after another of his dog in different poses and hats and so on. He's so proud of the dog that it's rather touching, but you can't help wondering whether he'd be as proud of his future offspring.

—NAOMI WATTS, actress

🐾 🐾 🐾

My friend Forrest had a dog called Peaches because she loved to eat peaches. She knew lots of tricks and was very smart. One day I was joking with Forrest. I said, "Do you think Peaches could learn to tell time?" I put my wrist out to Peaches, and she leaned her face right in to my watch. So I said, "Look, Peaches is trying to figure out what time it is!" Forrest was delighted. But I could see that Peaches was simply licking my watch's leather strap. After all, a dog is a dog.

—KAREN CARPENTER, singer and drummer

I would never ask someone to give up their pet. But I once broke up with a man I was fond of because his Irish Setter was jealous of me. The man was Irish American, by the way. Anyhow, it came down to either me or the darn dog . . . I chose not to come between the longtime pals and compatriots.
—ELIZABETH MONTGOMERY, actress (*Bewitched*)

A writer I know has a very affectionate, clingy dog that tries to sit in his lap whenever the writer sits down at his computer. He doesn't get as much work done as he'd like to, and he's not on staff, he's a freelancer.
—WAYNE WARGA, *Entertainment Tonight* writer

Dogs can be too jealous. Possessive. Cats don't have the same hang-ups. They don't cling.
—KAM FONG, actor (*Hawaii Five-O*)

My cat is fascinated by my computer. Now and then he'll try to work the mouse. One time, a neighbor's dog tried to eat the mouse.
—JERRY SEINFELD, actor and comedian

Cats are smarter than dogs. You can't get eight cats to pull a sled through snow.

—JEFF VALDEZ, writer and producer

I often tease my dog, who's a German Shepherd. I ask, "If you're a police dog, where's your badge? Huh? Where's your badge?" The unvarying answer is a confused sideward tilt of the head.

—JAMES THURBER, writer and cartoonist

I loathe people who keep dogs. They are cowards who haven't got the guts to bite people themselves.

—AUGUST STRINDBERG, playwright

Some four million Americans a year are bitten by dogs. Over two million of them are children.

—Dr. PHIL, talk-show host

After a dog bites you, often the owner will state it was just trying to be friendly. Hah! Whatever the cause, the result is the same—pain, anxiety, and possibly a lawsuit and rabies.

—FLORENCE BATES, lawyer turned actress (*Rebecca*)

Dogs can be pretty quick to bite. Not cats. They save it for when it's really needed. Dogs are promiscuous biters.

—WILL SMITH, actor

That old saying, "His bark is worse than his bite," is idiotic. They're both awful. Have you ever had to listen late at night to a dog barking—barking, barking, barking . . . they never get tired of barking.

—LUCY LIU, actress

When I was a kid I got a dog that my parents got rid of after a few weeks. I cried but tried to be mature. I asked *why*? They said because it barked. I said a dog can't talk, so it has to bark. They said but it barked too much. I said that I once heard Dad say Mom's mother had diarrhea of the mouth—and she'd been living with us for years.

—CARL MARTIN VERDUGO, columnist and zoologist

❧ ❧ ❧

Big dogs make an awful racket when they bark. Very annoying. You'd think it wouldn't be as bad with a small dog, but its yip-yip-yip-yip-yip-yip-yip-yip-yip can drive you crazy.

—ANN B. DAVIS, actress (*The Brady Bunch*)

❧ ❧ ❧

Dogs are outrageous extroverts. You could say cats are more moderate and considerate. Even in the sounds they make. One of my favorite lines is: "To err is human, to purr feline."

—MORGAN FAIRCHILD, actress and feline activist

❧ ❧ ❧

I wonder how true it is that dog people are more gregarious and cat people are more introverted? Or put it another way: that dog people are more insecure and cat ones are more independent? They should do a sociological study on this.

—LOUIE ANDERSON, comedian and host

Two cats pass on the street. They ignore each other, go their own way. Two leashed dogs meet up, and what a hubbub! One wants to have sex immediately. Or one insists that the other depart his territory. Or they want to kill each other. Isn't nature fun.

—DACK RAMBO, actor (*Dallas*)

It's a pity dogs, amongst other animals, have no idea when they're being used. By humans against other animals. One expects more from dogs—they're supposed to be affectionate. . . . What better example than people astride mindless galloping horses chasing after a pack of frenzied, blood-hungry dogs chasing one terrified fox in order to bite into it and tear it to pieces while still alive? All for the fun or "sport" of purported human beings.

—KEIRA KNIGHTLEY, actress

Fox hunting is the unspeakable in pursuit of the inedible.

—OSCAR WILDE, legendary writer and wit

If animals could speak, the dog would be a blundering, outspoken fellow but the cat would have the rare grace of never saying a word too much.

—MARK TWAIN, writer

I think if dogs could talk, they might be as difficult to deal with as people. . . . Language brings its own set of problems. It has nice words and bad words.

      —EVA LONGORIA, actress (*Desperate Housewives*)

🐾   🐾   🐾

The sad thing is when certain human beings take a dog, such as the Pit Bull, which in Europe it doesn't make headlines, and they transform it into something vicious. To mirror of course those certain vastly frightened or hateful human beings.

      —ISABELLE HUPPERT, actress

🐾   🐾   🐾

My granddaughter said something rather profound the other day. She said about their dog, "It's kind of sad that for a dog, his mouth is his hand."

      —RON HOWARD, actor turned director

🐾   🐾   🐾

Cats and dogs grow up so quickly, too quickly. It's marvelous for children to have pets. That is, until the pets start having children.

      —Dame MAGGIE SMITH, actress

People, it is *so* important to neuter and spay. . . . The other day a friend told me about birth control pills for dogs. Is this true? Or was she joking? She said it's part of the veterinary society's anti-litter campaign.

—ELAINE STRITCH, Broadway star

❀   ❀   ❀

An intact male dog is three times more likely to attack than a neutered dog.

—PAUL OWENS, dog trainer

❀   ❀   ❀

Dogs don't have a sense of shame about having sex anywhere, in front of anyone. You rarely see two cats having sex. Okay, you hear them, but they do like privacy.

—JENNIFER LAWRENCE, actress

❀   ❀   ❀

Dogs' behavior sometimes requires a tactful explanation. The small child of a friend once asked me why one dog was standing so closely behind another dog. I said, "The doggy in front is blind, and the other doggy has most kindly offered to push it all the way home."

—Sir NOEL COWARD, actor, playwright, director, and composer

Except when it came to hunting, dogs were less prized centuries ago than cats, which caught and destroyed rats. When a man was judged to be a rat or a low-down skunk, they labeled him a dirty dog. It's only since the Industrial Revolution, when people gained more leisure time and money, that dogs have become widely loved.

—Dr. MARGARET MEAD, anthropologist

The ancient Egyptians worshipped cats, not dogs. There was no dog goddess or god.

—SHARI LEWIS, ventriloquist

When you're Turkish, reading Shakespeare in English is terribly difficult, worse than for English people or Americans. I had been told in *Othello* there is a line about a "circumcised dog." I looked it up and was disappointed it was not an animal, but a "malignant and turbaned Turk." Shakespeare, who was Christian and uncircumcised, had a hatred of Muslims and Jews, who were and who are circumcised.

—MEHMET MURAT SOMER, author

And who can ever forget Mel Gibson's *Hamlet*—though many have tried. He's admitted he's eaten dog, and doesn't condemn the practice. Although I'm Japanese American, I'm willing to condemn the very few remaining people in Japan who eat small dogs, as well as the practice of eating dolphin meat there. Dolphins, like dogs and like humans, are mammals.

—GEORGE TAKEI, actor (*Star Trek*)

I once dated this guy, *once*, who in a Chinese restaurant said we really shouldn't judge if some Asians eat dogs because that's part of their culture. I told him slavery was once part of our culture and women not being able to vote or own property or attend college was part of culture and that sentient beings are not to be harmed in the name of culture. He didn't know what "sentient" meant.

—BONNIE FRANKLIN, actress (*One Day at a Time*)

A chap I went on a date with let slip in conversation that he was allergic to cats. I asked why one never hears of people being allergic to dogs? He didn't know either, but then he announced that dogs are cleaner than cats. Excuse me? Cats are by far the cleaner animal . . . and they bathe themselves. When dogs need baths it's usually up to the owners to do it for them.

—MICHELLE DOCKERY, actress (*Downton Abbey*)

Unlike some schoolmates, I didn't have the sort of parents who threatened to wash their children's mouths out with soap. So I didn't know what soap tasted like until I washed a dog.

—BENEDICT CUMBERBATCH, actor

🐾 🐾 🐾

Did you know in Islam the dog is considered unclean, but the cat isn't? I heard the reason is Mohammed had a pet cat but he didn't like dogs.

—PAULA ABDUL, singer

🐾 🐾 🐾

I don't own a dog, but for a long time I wondered why dogs have to be taken out and walked for their bathroom chores. I mean, children and cats can be house-broken . . . so might it be that dogs simply desire the extra time spent walking about with their owners? Maybe they don't want to learn . . . maybe they secretly want to hold on to the extra attention and quality time? I still wonder about this sometimes.

—JENNIFER SAUNDERS, actress and writer
(*Absolutely Fabulous*)

[This] baffles me, big-time . . . how dogs can learn so many more tricks than cats. Besides, dogs are so much more willing and eager to perform, to please their human masters. Yet dogs can't seem to learn how to go to the bathroom indoors, in their special place—you know, with like "doggy litter." Something any old cat can be trained to do. I don't get it.

—GREG PROOPS, comedian

I prefer a cat to a dog for the same reason I like a self-cleaning oven and a no-fuss vacuum cleaner. My schedule is hectic, I come and go. A cat does its business at home, a dog you have to be there to walk it a few times a day or get someone to do it for you. I'm not saying a dog isn't usually more outwardly affectionate than a cat, but hey, I hardly have time for a boyfriend. Anyway, affection is not high on my list of priorities.

—BARBARA COLBY, actress
(*The Mary Tyler Moore Show*)

Can you imagine being a dog-walker? If you like dogs' company a lot, that's one thing. Even so, it's pretty demeaning. A job where you're hired to take someone to go to the potty and then to clean up after it? How much lower could you stoop? Literally.

—BESS MYERSON, Miss America turned game-show
panelist and politician

🐾 🐾 🐾

I like dogs and cats about equally well. Each has its pros and cons . . . I've known very few people who hated dogs, but several who hate cats, and most strike me as immature and obsessive.

—HERMAN COHEN, producer
(I Was a Teenage Werewolf)

"My ladies" is what I call my dogs, who are a big and very positive part of my life. Yet I can understand people who are wary of dogs or indifferent to them. . . . What can be upsetting is the vehemence of certain dog lovers who dislike cats. Personally, I like cats. But certain dog people, you can almost guess that they're really talking about females, in which case those people—who most often are men—are the equivalent of male chauvinist pigs. Personally, I like pigs . . . the animal kind.

—NANCY KULP, actress (*The Beverly Hillbillies*)

Apartment dwellers have gotten more selfish and devious. They lie to get their way and not follow a rule other tenants follow. I refer to how easy it's become to get a fake certificate declaring that any dog is a so-called service dog. To get around the no-pets rule. It's like with the "handicapped" signs in cars, so people can get an easy parking space. Due to lies and abuse, the situation's gotten totally out of hand.

—WES CRAVEN, director

The worst is "service dog" owners who defy you, who even threaten you with a lawsuit if you dare ask if it's really a service dog or want to see its papers. Most people back down too easily against these aggressive jerks. . . . Another thing: true service dogs are trained to bark minimally. So if it's a noisy dog, it's not a service dog, and you should have your landlord take action. Of course there are landlords and landlords.

—MICHAEL MASSEE, actor (*The Crow*)

I had a downstairs neighbor whose dog barked. Too much. . . . The building owner refused to get involved. He lived elsewhere and didn't have to listen to this mutt, whose owner was a pain. My complaints to her had no effect. I'm a writer and a night owl. So I took to exercising on my machines at two, three, four in the morning. Waking up the below-stairs neighbor. Tit for tat. It worked. Her dog barked much less thereafter. You've got to fight fire with fire.

—EDWARD L. BEACH JR., novelist and
submarine pioneer

When I was growing up, I thought my dog was real smart and the neighbor kid was a dummy. Mostly 'cause my dog followed me wherever I went and the neighbor didn't pay any attention to me. Now I wish I'd paid more attention to what my dog wanted to do and made more of an effort with the neighbor. He grew up to be a tycoon.

—SKIP E. LOWE, cable TV talk-show host

My mom thought Chihuahuas were too "breakable." I wanted to get one when I grew up. I grew up and a friend told me her neighbor had a Chihuahua until it got stolen. A few years later I heard of another Chihuahua kidnapping. They're so cute, everyone wants one, legally or not. I couldn't bear to love an animal and then just have it snatched out of my life.

—MADELINE KAHN, actress

Okay, Chihuahuas are adorable. And those imploring Mexican eyes . . . but for me, they're too jittery to live with, day in and day out. I can admire or desire a certain person or dog and still realize they're not for me on a 24/7 basis. An affair with a vapid blonde or an afternoon with a nervous little dog might be fun, but I couldn't live with either.

—CARLOS MENCIA, comedian

I've always thought Chihuahuas are little charmers. I still do. But after I read a library book on rearing them . . . good grief! All the things you're supposed not to do! Many of them because those little dogs are so fragile. They require a lot of care and caution and maintenance . . . and it's for a lifetime. At least kids eventually take care of themselves—or better yet, move out.

—LARRY HAGMAN, actor (*Dallas*)

❖   ❖   ❖

Despite her size, Chiquita, our first Chihuahua, was sturdy, had a big personality, and we only lost her at sixteen. But I still never thought the breed was for me. . . . The object of my affections is my now two-pound Chihuahua, Minnie Mouse, who is the most adorable, lovable dog I've had yet. And the breed is even better than I thought. There's a reason why you see so many Chihuahuas now—they are smart, fun, easy to take care of, and endearing in many ways. She warms my heart and makes me laugh.

—DANIELLE STEELE, author of a nonfiction book about
Minnie and her other dogs titled *Pure Joy*

I cannot see the attraction of Bulldogs. They can't help being ugly, but have you ever smelled one's breath? As to background, they were bred to bite into and clamp down on a bull until it finally died of blood loss and exhaustion. I'd find almost any other breed preferable.

—HOWARD ROLLINS, actor

       🐾   🐾   🐾

I didn't particularly want a dog. I had a cat and was happy with her. But I was often away and she seemed depressed at times. She was a young cat. Then I babysat a dog for a friend for two days. My cat and the dog got along great. Never mind what you see in cartoons. My cat was perkier and seemed happier, so I asked my friend if she would consider selling me her dog. She said she'd been offered a better job up north but was hesitating 'cause she'd be living with her elderly mother who didn't think dogs belonged inside a house. My offer freed my friend up to move, and my cat got a friend and an improved personality.

—BUTTERFLY MCQUEEN, actress (*Gone with the Wind*)

I wouldn't want one of those mostly-for-show breeds like a Saluki or those Italian Wolfhounds, etc. They're painfully thin, like anorexic. They're rare and fun to look at. But those spindly shanks [legs] . . . the least pressure might break them. And to walk such a dog—everyone would be staring at the dog and the owner. No. Too psychologically demanding.

—RICKY GERVAIS, actor and comedian

🐾 🐾 🐾

I've seen dogs eat standing up even in one-dog households with no competition. They stand because their pack-animal ancestors competed for the dead meat and didn't get any if they tried to sit and eat. . . . Two of my friends have cats that eat sitting down. In the wild, cats are solitary hunters and don't have to compete. They can afford to sit and eat. Which definitely looks more civilized. I also think hunting is more fair when it's one on one, not a pack against a lone animal.

—ALAN YOUNG, actor (*Mr. Ed*)

It's not fair to blame dogs for over-populating! They don't have human intelligence, and even humans over-populate. The poorest humans usually have the most kids. That's intelligence? It's up to humans to do for their dogs. Like the bumper sticker says: If Your Pet Won't Wear a Condom, Get Him Fixed!

—SHARON GLESS, actress (*Cagney and Lacey*)

I don't get how "bitch," which originally just meant a female dog, became such a put-down word against female humans. . . . And when you call a man a son-of-a-bitch, you're insulting his mother more than him. It's ridiculously and mindlessly unfair.

—UMA THURMAN, actress

In a movie, someone called the protagonist a clever dog. I'd have thought it was a compliment, but the way it was said I could tell it wasn't. Somehow, a clever dog isn't smart or admirable, he's sneaky or underhanded. Go figure.

—DAVID BRENNER, comedian

Last week I heard a guy in the park tell another guy, "I love all dogs." To me, that's dumb, it's sappy—like he was trying to impress. It's like saying, "I love all people." There are all kinds of dogs and all kinds of people. Some are lovable but many for sure are not.

—JAMES FRANCO, actor and filmmaker

🐾 🐾 🐾

No wonder they call it a pet peeve. . . . My pet peeve is two sorts of dog owners. The ones who don't mind that their dog barks a lot and won't try to restrain it, like the parents of little girls who love to scream. Also the ones who, when their dog barks at you or it lunges at you but thank goodness he's on a leash, they either say, "He's just saying hello" or "He's just trying to be friendly." I say, See you in court, friendly people!

—MOREY AMSTERDAM, comedian
(*The Dick Van Dyke Show*)

If a human being barked—or yelled—as long as some dogs do at night, he'd be hoarse. Or ruin his vocal chords. . . . A doctor friend who isn't a veterinarian explained that the human larynx is more fragile than a canine one. A dog's doesn't get damaged as easily. A dog larynx is stronger but has a narrower range of sound. A trade-off, I suppose.

—Sir DEREK JACOBI, actor

❄ ❄ ❄

People ooh and ah over little dogs. It's a size thing. Have you ever lived with a little dog? Or very near one? Little doesn't necessarily mean sweet or passive. Sometimes they have a Napoleon complex. They can be insecure, neurotic, and loud—relatively—and aggressive toward bigger dogs. Their life's about trying to prove something. Like a short boyfriend I once had.

—MARY WILSON, singer, formerly of The Supremes

❄ ❄ ❄

It's really interesting to see the way two dogs interact. It gives us a better perspective on how we ourselves behave. Or misbehave.

—ADAM SANDLER, actor and producer

Dogs hate each other even worse than people do each other. Two dogs meet in the street, they typically want to attack each other sexually or just attack each other.

—SACHA BARON COHEN, actor

* * *

Don't ever try to break up a fight between two dogs. I've seen it happen, and every expert will tell you the only thing you'll break up is the surface of your skin, and worse.

—DESI ARNAZ JR., former actor and son of Lucille Ball

* * *

Dog love can come between people. It did with two of my schoolmates, fraternal [not identical] twins. Their parents gave them a French Poodle for their birthday. All was well until it came time to get the Poodle's fur trimmed and styled. The two couldn't and wouldn't agree, or even compromise, on what the dog should look like. They didn't speak for almost a month. Admittedly, in the end it wasn't really about dog love.

—WILLIAM COMO, editor of *After Dark* magazine

There was a hairstyle fad called the Poodle Cut that came along in the 1950s, out of Europe. Short hair that was supposed to look stylish, boyish, and feminine, all at the same time. Well, it may have suited a Poodle, but most of the famous women who made it popular were simply too old for it—fooling themselves and looking stylishly foolish.

—AUDREY MEADOWS, actress (*The Honeymooners*)

❖   ❖   ❖

I attended an early-1990s lunch meeting at the Ma Maison hotel in West Hollywood. It's gone now, but I was astonished when they said I couldn't take my leftovers home in a doggie bag. Why not? They said it was unsanitary, then cleared the plates away before I could finish the food! I really should have protested . . . I sometimes enjoy having midnight snacks out of a doggie bag. If I don't particularly like what I've brought home, I save it for the neighbor's cat. Her name's Micki—she eats anything. Including mice.

—ELIZABETH WILSON, actress (*Nine to Five*)

Cats are quiet. Cats do not make you feel guilty. And they do not wake you up in the morning. But if you want or require a false sense of power and constant reassurance from a dumb animal that you're wise and wonderful, then clearly a dog is right for you.

—LEON AMES, actor

❦   ❦   ❦

People prefer either-or answers. When I lectured in Northern Ireland I immediately informed the audience, so as to offend neither Catholics nor Protestants, that I was an atheist. A woman raised her hand. "But would it be the Protestants' or the Catholics' God you're not believin' in?" In the same vein, in New York City, where I'm never seen with an animal, I am often asked which I prefer—cats or dogs? I hesitate to take sides, but who ever said I liked either?

—QUENTIN CRISP, author and wit

Epilogue

One day before delivering this manuscript to my editor I happened upon the January 2017 issue of *The Pet Press*, which is free and a labor of love via longtime publisher and editor Lori Golden. Its cover featured actress Loretta Swit, best known from *M*A*S*H*. On the eve of being honored by Actors and Others for Animals, Swit emphasized the importance of spaying and neutering. Due to pet overpopulation, somewhere between three and four million animals (according to the Humane Society of the United States) or nine and eleven million animals (per shelter manager Al Ramirez, AlleyCat ALF) are annually "put to sleep" in shelters.

Swit pointed out that within six to eight years one unspayed animal may engender some eighty thousand offspring . . . and also that a single fur coat may take the lives of about seventy-five animals. (She added that faux furs are cheaper, don't require storage, don't smell in the rain, and are twice as warm.)

The actress and activist also mentioned her rescue dogs, "the best breed there is."

Two days before delivering this manuscript, I met Greg Schreiner, founder and president of MarilynRemembered.org, the leading Marilyn Monroe website and fan club. My book prior to this one was all about MM, who animal advocates like Betty White, Earl Holliman, and Brigitte Bardot believe would have become an animal-rights activist had she survived Hollywood.

Mr. Schreiner introduced me to two of his three rescue dogs, all female Dachshunds. One had suffered abuse and was initially wary of me and never came that close. When I commented that she sounded hoarse, Greg said the previous owners had cut her vocal cords. Why? "They said she barked too much."

The unabused rescue was as affectionate as could be, parking on my lap and bestowing repeated licks and kisses. The third Dachshund, who'd been especially abused, I didn't meet—she avoids humans and is even shy of her "sister" dogs, habitually seeking security alone in another room.

Rescues are a rewarding and humanitarian option for dog lovers, who can provide the innocent, vulnerable pooches with a loving, caring home and a happy ending. By contrast, to learn a lot about the $11 billion industry of selling dogs and how they're treated—including puppy mills and high-kill "shelters," a sadly misleading word—read Kim Kavin's recent and riveting book *The Dog Merchants*.

Because most puppies, like babies, become less cute as they grow older or because dogs bark or tear up gardens or incur costly veterinary bills, hundreds of thousands of dogs a year are dropped off at shelters and humane societies, often in the belief that more suitable homes will be found for them— that there are enough big-hearted people out there who will rescue them. Shelter manager Al Ramirez informed *The Pet Press*, "There's a 90 percent chance that a dog will never walk out of the shelter it's dumped at," including purebreds.

Al's wish is that anyone who has ever "surrendered" a dog work just one day in the *back* of an animal shelter, where a dog usually has seventy-two hours to find a new home or die: "Your pet will be confined to a small run/kennel in a room with other barking or crying animals. It will have to relieve itself where it eats and sleeps. It will be depressed and it will cry constantly for the family that abandoned it."

If no one comes to the rescue, the dog "will be taken from its kennel on a leash. They always look like they think they are going for a walk—happy, wagging their tails. Until they get to The Room, when every one of them freaks out and puts on the brakes when we get to the door. It must smell like death or they can feel the sad souls that are left in there. It's strange, but it happens with every one of them."

Before you or a friend or relative purchases a puppy or a new dog, please consider a rescue dog. They're free, and only you can free them and let them live.

And please don't forget to spay and neuter.

Index